1 0 0

*F*AVORITE

*H*ERBS

100 FAVORITE HERBS

TERI DUNN

MetroBooks

DEDICATION

Dedicated to Sarah Bollinger, wonderful friend and chef extraordinaire

(you make the best cream-of-sorrel soup!).

Thanks to Susan Lauzau, Robert and Florence Sacks, Christine Dobek, Janet H.

Sanchez, Kathleen Pyle, Larry Maxcy, all our wonderful neighbors on 37th and

Raymond—and Shawn and Wes. Special thanks to Tristan, for waiting!

MetroBooks

An Imprint of Friedman/Fairfax Publishers

© 1998 by Michael Friedman Publishing Group, Inc.

Library of Congress Cataloging-in-Publication Data available upon request.

ISBN 1-56799-526-8

Editors: Susan Lauzau and Rachel Simon
Art Director: Lynne Yeamans
Designer: Milagros Sensat
Photography Editor: Amy Talluto
Production Director: Karen Matsu Greenberg

Color separations by Ocean Graphic Co. Ltd.
Printed in Singapore by KHL Printing Co Ltd.

For bulk purchases and special sales, please contact:
Friedman/Fairfax Publishers
Attention: Sales Department
15 West 26th Street
New York, NY 10010
212/685-6610 FAX 212/685-1307

Visit our website:
http://www.metrobooks.com

Photography credits:

©Scooter Cheatham: p. 81

Envision: ©George Livadras: pp. 25, 35, ©George Mattei: pp. 32, 43, 52, 92, ©Emily Johnson: p. 60

©Derek Fell: pp. 12, 13, 20, 36, 61, 65, 74, 100, 102, 104, 106, 114, 115

©John Glover: pp. 2 and 112 (Garden Design by Fairfield Sorrey Herb Garden / Wild Life Pond)

©Jessie M. Harris: p. 30

©Dency Kane: pp. 10, 11, 15, 23, 24, 27, 29, 40, 41, 42, 44, 48, 51, 56, 57, 59, 62, 69, 71, 73, 77, 78, 80, 82, 84, 85, 87, 88, 89, 94, 95, 101, 105, 108, 111, 116

©Charles Mann: pp. 19, 64

©Clive Nichols: pp. 7 (East Lambrook Manor, Somerset), 34 (Sticky Wicket, Dorset), 47 (The Anchorage, Kent), 93 (Design by Rupert Golby-Chelsea 95)

©Jerry Pavia: pp. 16, 17, 18, 21, 26, 28, 31, 39, 46, 58, 63, 66, 67, 68, 70, 72, 75, 86, 90, 91, 97, 99, 107, 109, 110, 117

©Joanne Pavia: pp. 14, 33, 38, 53, 55, 76, 83, 98, 103, 113

Photo/Nats: ©Ann Reilly p. 22, ©David M. Stone p. 37, ©Betsy Fuchs p. 45, ©Ben Phillips p. 96

©Andy Van Hevelingen: pp. 49, 79

©Visuals Unlimited: ©D. Cavagnaro p. 50, ©Robert W. Domm p. 54

DISCLAIMER

While many herbal remedies have been used safely for years, even hundreds of years, inexperience can be dangerous. Improper or excessive doses of certain herbs can cause allergic or even toxic reactions. For these reasons, the author has been conservative in describing uses. Neither the author nor the publisher will be held responsible for any adverse reactions.

CONTENTS

Introduction

The world of herbs is both highly intriguing and somewhat daunting to the uninitiated. Yes, it's true that most herbs are quite easy to grow. Some are fast-growing annuals; some are long-lived perennials. Yes, many are grown primarily for their foliage, which is often deliciously scented. And many, many herbs are useful in the kitchen, adding an exciting new dimension to all sorts of recipes.

But you may have your reservations. Are all herbs dryland natives, and therefore best grown by those fortunate enough to live in a mild climate? (No, not at all, although the ones that are naturally tough can become low-maintenance stars in your garden.) Are herbs really glorified weeds that will take over your yard? (A few are rampant growers, but with wise planting and care, no herb need become a pest. Instead, you can plan for bountiful harvests.) What about safety—hasn't modern science discovered that many old herbal remedies are actually dangerous? (Many herbs have indeed been scrutinized by modern chemists and the medical world. Some are as helpful as touted; others are not. Appropriate cautions are noted in individual entries.)

Ultimately, perhaps the most common beginner's question is: just what is an herb? For the purposes of this book, an herb is broadly defined as a plant that not only has ornamental merits, but is also useful in some way. It may be edible—eaten fresh or dried, or added to any number of tasty recipes. It may be medicinal or have cosmetic properties. It may be useful in crafts or it may be a dye plant.

The truth is, the concerns that inexperienced herb gardeners have are unfounded. There are so many herbs that there is sure to be something for everyone, no matter what your taste or where you live. This book embraces a wide range of appealing herbs. Each entry should provide you with sufficient information about whether you can grow a given herb in your area and in the conditions available in your garden. (Not all herbs are simple to grow, but I have not included those with really exacting requirements.)

Shopping for Herbs

If you are lucky, you live near a garden center that has a good selection of herb plants, but you will usually only be able to find such common ones as parsley, sage, rosemary, and thyme. Some herbs enjoy a double life as perennial-garden flowers, and may be found in another part of the store or greenhouse. If you find what you are looking for, take a moment to examine the plant carefully before you buy it. Not only should it look healthy (no damaged or diseased leaves, no sign of lurking insects), it should be well rooted. Test the plant by turning it on its side or upside down and gently tapping the pot; if potting mix spills or the plant falls away, it's not a good choice. The best herbs are clearly growing vigorously, perhaps with some healthy white roots starting to quest out from the pot's bottom. These will transplant easily to your garden and grow eagerly, provided you've prepared a spot for them and care for them as they make the transition.

Another way to get good herb plants is to raise them from seed. Many grow easily and quickly in flats started indoors, and take off when you plant them outdoors after the soil has warmed up and danger of frost has passed. Some don't like to be transplanted and prefer to be sown directly in the garden. Read the seed packet carefully so you'll know best how to proceed.

If you are disappointed in the local selections, by all means shop for your herbs by mail. Perhaps even more so than for perennials, mail-order catalogs offer a huge range of herbal choices (but check their substitution policies in the event that they run out of something special you had your heart set on). And if herbs are their specialty, the catalogs often feature detailed descriptions that include cultivation information, snippets of folklore, and enticing suggestions for use. A list of mail-order companies is included at the end of this book.

Planting Herbs

No matter what kind of soils or sun exposures your yard offers, there's bound to be some herbs you can grow. You can always tuck a few into a flower border. For example, those with handsome foliage, like the sages, keep the display interesting when their neighbors are not in bloom; those with pretty flowers, such as calendula and nasturtium, are always welcome. Culinary herbs—especially basil and parsley—are often added to a vegetable garden.

Herbs can also be landscaping problem-solvers. If a corner has perpetually damp soil, why not plant it with mints? If you have a stone pathway or terrace, fragrant creeping thyme set in the cracks will soon scent the air and look like it has been there forever. If you'd like a pretty and low-maintenance edging plant, try lavender, germander, or rosemary.

As for planned herb gardens, there's no real secret to their design or success. You just have to prepare an area in advance by pulling out all the weeds and improving the soil if necessary. Formal layouts, like "knot gardens" or pie designs, should be planned on paper first. Use a dependable edging plant or bricks, stones, or wood to lay out the lines. As for the filler plants, just be sure you take into account their mature size so that you don't crowd them.

Some herb gardeners enjoy making "theme gardens," gardens devoted completely to one kind of herb or one concept. Popular themes include fragrance, dried flower, dye, herbal tea, medicinal, biblical, Shakespeare, and kitchen gardens. After you've carefully chosen appropriate plants, you can make the layout as artistic or informal as you wish. Just remember to allow yourself room to get in among the plants to groom, water, and harvest them.

CARING FOR HERBS

Each herb has its own cultural requirements, but some generalizations can still be made as you ponder getting started. Most herbs prefer full sun. Most prosper in good, moderately fertile soil. And most require that the soil be well drained so that they get the moisture they need to grow but don't suffer from "wet feet." If your chosen site is lacking in any of these requirements, take steps to improve it. Clip back overhanging shrubs and tree branches. Add organic matter, dampened peat moss, and/or sand to poor soil to improve its texture.

Plant your young herb plants on a cool day so that they don't have to cope with heat stress. A drizzly late-spring afternoon (after danger of frost has passed) is ideal. Pop the plant out of the pot or flat, tease loose some of the roots, and gently set the herb into an ample hole. Pat soil back in around it and water it well. Water your herb plant often in the following days and weeks until it becomes well established.

Fertilizer, on the other hand, is not often needed. Excess fertilizer may lead to lax, floppy growth that is unattractive and vulnerable to diseases and pests, and may also inhibit flowering. It's better to plant your herbs in the type of soil they are known to prefer, and leave it at that. However, an exception is made for lime lovers: if your garden soil is too acidic for an herb, a sprinkling of lime powder or chips at its base at planting time may be in order.

It's fun to raise some herbs in pots to place on a deck or patio, in a window box, or on a windowsill indoors. Some herbs are too tender to leave outdoors year-round, and must be grown indoors or in greenhouse conditions. In any event, start off with a good sterile soil mix. Sterile mixes are preferable simply because insect pests are not lurking in them, and sometimes indoor-grown herbs are vulnerable.

HARVESTING, DRYING AND STORING HERBS

Again, every herb is different, but some generalizations can be made about harvesting your crops. Wait until a plant is growing well—late summer or, if it's a perennial, even the second season—before clipping off leaves or flowers for your own use. Otherwise, you may set the plant back considerably or even unintentionally kill it. Go for the outer leaves first, if you can, as they tend to be the youngest and most tender. Flowers are best harvested not long after they've opened. Flavor, scent, and texture are at their peak in the morning, before the heat of the day sets in.

The right timing is always key when you're harvesting flowers, flower heads, or pods for drying, either for craft projects or in order to collect edible seeds. You want the flowers to have just opened and the seeds to be ripe, so keep a sharp eye out. For seeds, the best time to intervene is late summer, just as the plant begins to go brown or yellow but before it sheds its seeds on the ground.

Clip and hang clumps upside down in a dark, dry, windless spot, such as a shed, garage, enclosed porch, cellar, or attic. If seeds are likely to fall of their own accord, place a piece of white paper or a tarp below. Otherwise, wait until everything is dry, then pluck off your harvest. In the case of flower heads that "shatter" readily, place the harvest in a paper bag so that the seeds will be easily collected. Hard seed cases may need a good whack with a plastic baseball bat or a run under a rolling pin to give up their treats.

While the gradual drying method helps herbs retain more of their color, shape, scent, and flavor, some herbs can be dried efficiently using faster modern methods. Place the leaves or seeds on a clean cookie sheet and dry them for a few hours in the oven, set on low, with the door ajar to provide a little air circulation. Or, dry them briefly on paper towels in the microwave. To avoid scorching, dry them for ten to twenty seconds at a time, on low, until you reach the desired crispness. With the oven and microwave techniques, don't overlap—let individual pieces dry separately.

In any case, when the drying process is finished, winnow out unwanted plant parts such as seed cases, stalks, twigs, and leaves.

Fresh herbs usually don't last long once they're picked, so harvest them as close to mealtime as is practical or refrigerate them separately and add them just prior to serving. To keep them longer than a day, place the stalks (not the whole herb) in an inch or two (2.5 or 5cm) of water, and cover the jar, bowl, or bottle loosely and store it in the refrigerator. Or, wash and thoroughly dry your harvest, then lay it on dry paper towels with no overlapping before rolling up the paper towels and storing in a plastic bag in the vegetable crisper.

Dried herb leaves, flowers, and seeds often contain volatile oils that give them their wonderful scent and flavor. Make the most of your homegrown harvest by preserving these qualities. Always store your harvest in airtight jars or bags, out of direct sunlight, in a cool place.

COOKING WITH HERBS

Make the most of homegrown herbs by using the flavor at its peak. Generally speaking, fresh herbs are best kept whole until just prior to being added to a recipe, when you can quickly chop or dice them with a sharp knife or even tear them into small pieces by hand. Food processors and blenders sometimes do too good a job, making tiny pieces whose flavor has literally been beaten out of them.

As for dried or powdered herbs, some give back rich, aromatic flavor when simmered with a recipe for hours, while others are at their best if added in the last few minutes before serving. Follow the recipe's recommendations, or if there are none, experiment to see what suits your taste.

Agrimony

Agrimonia eupatoria

HEIGHT/WIDTH: 2'–5' ×1½' (60–150cm × 45cm)

FLOWERS/BLOOM TIME: yellow spikes/early summer

ZONES: 3–7

RECOMMENDED USES: medicinal, dye

Agrimony

Not an especially distinctive-looking plant, agrimony has nonetheless been prized for centuries in its native Europe. The serrated, aromatic leaves have many uses, though they are not considered edible. A mild tea made from a few teaspoons of dried leaves may be used to ease a sore throat or settle an upset stomach, or you can toss some into a warm bath to soothe aching muscles. A poultice applied to cuts and sores may also bring relief and faster healing. More elaborate claims are made about agrimony's benefits, including reducing bleeding and helping to heal problems with internal organs, but you should not try these remedies without the supervision of a professional herbalist or your family doctor. Finally, a dye made from leaves and stems will be yellow; the later you wait in the season to harvest, the darker the yellow.

The plant gains a certain willowy grace when in bloom. Blooming, tapered spikes rise a foot or two (30 or 60cm) above the leaves and are composed of tiny yellow flowers that wave in the breeze. Later, they become burrs. The whole plant wafts a soft aroma that has been likened to the scent of ripe apricots. Agrimony grows best in full sun to light shade in soil that's on the dry side, and will self-seed.

Aloe vera

Aloe barbadensis

HEIGHT/WIDTH: 1'–2' × 1'–2' (30–60cm × 30–60cm)

FLOWERS/BLOOM TIME: not grown for flowers/rarely seen

ZONES: 10 (elsewhere, grow as a houseplant)

RECOMMENDED USES: medicinal, cosmetic

Aloe

While many herbs never receive wide use or the blessing of the medical establishment, aloe stands out as a popular and effective plant. The fact that it's simple to grow certainly helps. An aloe plant will thrive despite minimal water, gritty soil, and part-day sun on a windowsill almost anywhere. In fact, this ancient plant, said to be native to Africa, seems to prosper on neglect, developing little "pup" plants at its base in a matter of months. Dividing and repotting is simple, and the gift of an aloe plant is always welcome.

When you snap off one of aloe's fleshy leaves, both sides immediately bleed a sticky sap that brings quick relief to itchy skin, minor kitchen burns, sunburns, cuts, and abrasions. Often, once healed, no scar remains. The cosmetic industry has extracted and repackaged this healing gel in many over-the-counter treatments that ease itching and pain and keep the skin soft and supple. If you don't have this valuable plant on your kitchen sill now, you should get one.

Angelica

Angelica archangelica

HEIGHT/WIDTH: 3′–8′ × 1′–2′ (90–240cm × 30-60cm)

FLOWERS/BLOOM TIME: greenish white umbels/early to midsummer

ZONES: 4–9

RECOMMENDED USES: medicinal, cosmetic, culinary

Angelica

An intriguing plant with a long and colorful history, angelica is not for every garden. It grows quite tall, eventually towering over its neighbors. It may not flower its first year. When in bloom, its wonderful scent—sweet and aniselike—may attract clouds of fruit flies and blackflies. And in or out of bloom, deer love to nibble it to the ground.

Having said all that, angelica's good qualities should be noted. It's a good-looking ornamental plant, sporting attractive, long-lasting flower heads and tropical-looking leaves on handsome, hollow stalks. The stalks have traditionally been harvested and sugared for use as a sweet snack, or diced and added to cakes, especially fruitcakes. Raw or sautéed, the stalks are served as a celery- or asparaguslike side dish in some countries. A soothing tea used primarily in the treatment of bronchial ailments can be made from the leaves. Angelica is also used as a flavoring in vermouth, gin, and the liqueur Chartreuse, and the entire plant is aromatic.

The plant gets its evocative name from an old legend that the archangel Michael appeared in a vision to a seventeenth-century monk, revealing angelica as a remedy against various ills, especially the Black Plague.

Angelica is best started from seed sown directly in the garden, in rich, moist soil. It will prosper beautifully in partial shade.

Anise

Pimpinella anisum

HEIGHT/WIDTH: 12″–24″ × 8″ (30–60cm × 20cm)

FLOWERS/BLOOM TIME: white umbels/mid- to late summer

ZONES: best in warmer areas (annual)

RECOMMENDED USES: culinary, medicinal

Anise

If you love the elegant flavor and aroma of licorice, this herb is the most refined source. However, you will mainly be after the seeds, and the plant takes three to four months to go to seed. So gardeners with long summers have the best luck (the rest of us can try starting plants from seed indoors in late winter). And be forewarned: what catnip is to cats, anise is to some dogs.

Anise is a pretty, lacy plant, with flattened, creamy white umbel flowers. It has heart-shaped to roundish leaves down low and more feathery ones higher on the stalk. Don't overlook using the leaves—they're nice in garden-fresh salads or minced and added to soft cheese dips or spreads. The seeds should be harvested when almost ripe (turning brown) and used whole or ground. Anise is splendid in everything from stewed fruit desserts and chutneys to soups, meat dishes, and steamed vegetables as well as breads, cakes, and cookies. It has a long history as a digestive aid, which is why it is popular in after-dinner liqueurs and teas. It also enjoys a reputation as a breath freshener and is sometimes an ingredient in cough suppressants, though more for its pleasant taste than for any remarkable expectorant qualities. Grow anise in average soil in full sun.

Anise hyssop

Agastache foeniculum

HEIGHT/WIDTH: $2'–4' \times 2'$ (60–120cm $\times$ 60cm)

FLOWERS/BLOOM TIME: violet-purple spikes/mid- to late summer

ZONES: 4–9

RECOMMENDED USES: culinary, craft

Anise hyssop

Despite its name, this handsome herb is neither an anise nor a hyssop, but a member of the mint family. Thus it has the characteristic square stem of mints and a preference for fertile, well-drained soil. Give anise hyssop full sun or partial shade. A cool, minty flavor with anise overtones makes for a pleasantly tangy scent and taste.

The plant grows erect and has nice dark green leaves. These are joined later in the summer by lovely violet-purple spires that produce lots of nectar, attracting hummingbirds and bees. In fact, anise hyssop is sometimes grown commercially to aid honey production. For the purposes of the home gardener, however, the dried leaves can be used to make a tasty hot or iced tea. A strong brew of the liquid can also be added to favorite recipes as a sweetener. Both the leaves and the flowers hold their color and scent well in potpourris, dried bouquets, and wreaths.

Basil

Ocimum basilicum

HEIGHT/WIDTH: $2' \times 1'$ (60cm $\times$ 30cm)

FLOWERS/BLOOM TIME: white whorls/late summer

ZONES: all zones (frost-sensitive annual)

RECOMMENDED USES: culinary

Few herbs are as widely used as this one—for who can resist fragrant, delicious basil? It enhances the flavor of sauces as well as many main dishes, especially in Italian and Asian cooking. Most popular is the bushy sweet basil, with its large, somewhat crinkly leaves. Plant it in full sun in fertile soil. The secret to a long and abundant harvest of leaves is to clip or pinch off the unremarkable flowers as soon as they appear. Regular harvesting of the leaves will also help keep the plant more compact.

You'll find that fresh leaves have much more flavor than dried. Roll excess leaves (cleaned and completely dry) in paper towels and freeze them in plastic bags. Basil is the major ingredient in the classic Italian pesto sauce, which doesn't freeze as well as plain basil leaves. It still tastes good once thawed, but loses its vibrant green color.

There's a broad range of related basils, available primarily from mail-order seed companies. All are worth

Basil

experimenting with—they'll contribute a slightly different color or form to your garden, and there are flavor variations for all sorts of dishes. Look for lemon basil, which is a wonderful addition to fish recipes or a refreshing summer gazpacho. There are also cinnamon, licorice, and Thai basils. The pert little rounded plants of 'Spicy Globe' basil sport tiny but still flavorful leaves, and make a unique, easy-care edging plant—even in a flower garden.

Any of the basils can be grown indoors on a window sill, though they must be constantly pinched back to keep a bushy form. Full sun will also prevent the plants from becoming too rangy.

Basil thyme

Calamintha nepeta

HEIGHT/WIDTH: 12″–24″ × 8″–12″ (30–60cm × 20–30cm)

FLOWERS/BLOOM TIME: light purple/summer

ZONES: 5–9

RECOMMENDED USES: culinary

Basil thyme

This pleasant herb is not always easy to find, but it is easy to grow and easy to love (your best bet is to seek it out in specialty herb catalogs).

The emerald green leaves are ridged and have bluntly serrated edges, looking quite a bit like mint leaves. They grow in whorls around the stem like mint (in fact, it is more closely related to mint than to basil or thyme). The pretty flowers, which vary from pink to lilac, are produced over a long season, making the plant an attractive addition to an herb garden or flower border. Basil thyme is never troubled by pests or diseases. It thrives in average to damp soil and full sun. If you cut it back every month or two during the summer, it stays neat-looking. In any case, it never gets very large, making it suitable for smaller spaces.

You can use the clipped leaves to make a sweet-flavored, aromatic tea. In Europe, where it is a common weed, it has been used to sweeten preserved meats and to treat everything from colic to fever.

Bay

Laurus nobilis

HEIGHT/WIDTH: 25′–60′ × 10′–20′ (7.5–18m 3 3-6m);

    in a pot, 5′–10′ × 3′–5′ (150–300cm × 90–150cm)

FLOWERS/BLOOM TIME: small yellow clusters/early

    summer

ZONES: 8–10

RECOMMENDED USES: culinary, craft

Bay

This "herb" is actually a tree, and gardeners who must have one can always try growing it in a large pot, which will help keep the size more manageable. Just be sure to place it where it won't be tossed about by drying winds, water it regularly through the growing season, and protect it from winter cold. The potting mix can be soil-based as long as it drains well (make sure that there's a hole in the bottom of the pot).

Bay is a handsome plant, with smooth tan to gray bark, slender, pungent leaves, and inconspicuous flowers that are followed by small purple-black drupes (stone fruits, like cherries). The leaves are the main attraction, and have been prized by cooks the world over because they impart their fragrant oils to food gradually. This is why bay so enhances the flavor of slowly simmered soups, stews, and meats as well as bottled vinegars and homemade pickles. Bay is also a major ingredient in bouquet garni, a mixture that originated in France and traditionally includes thyme and parsley. Bay's sturdy dried branches make a good base for a wreath or swag, though the leaves fade somewhat.

Bee balm

Monarda didyma

HEIGHT/WIDTH: $2\frac{1}{2}'$–$4' \times 1\frac{1}{2}'$ (75–120cm $\times$ 45cm)

FLOWERS/BLOOM TIME: showy flower heads/mid- to late summer

ZONES: 4–9

RECOMMENDED USES: craft, culinary, medicinal.

Bee balm

This showy plant is popular with perennial gardeners, thanks to its large, vibrant flowers (in shades of red, pink, purple, and white), but it is also worth the notice of herb gardeners. As a member of the mint family, bee balm has the fragrant foliage you'd expect—minty, with a sunny, orange-lemon tang.

Added to summertime beverages such as iced tea, lemonade, and sangria, bee balm leaves contribute zing (steep them first for best results). Both leaves and flowers also make a nice garnish for these drinks or for fresh salads. Brewed as a hot tea, bee balm is said to ease cold symptoms, nausea, and cramps, although these uses have not been veri-fied by scientific research. At any rate, the plant is perfectly harmless.

To grow this plant well, you must give it rich, moist soil in full sun or partial shade, and perhaps spray for mildew late in the summer (it is very susceptible). Do not eat leaves that have been sprayed.

Potpourri fanciers also enjoy adding bee balm to their mixtures. The flower heads are really clusters of small tubular flowers that, with a little encouragement, shatter when dried. They tend to lose a little bit of their color, so use the brightest cultivars such as 'Cambridge Scarlet' and 'Gardenview Scarlet' for this purpose.

Bergamot

Monarda punctata

HEIGHT/WIDTH: 12″–18″ × 8″–12″ (30–45cm × 20–30cm)

FLOWERS/BLOOM TIME: yellowish with purple spots/summer

ZONES: 4–9

RECOMMENDED USES: culinary, medicinal

Bergamot

This is the monarda sometimes seen in wild fields and meadows. It is less showy than its garden cousin, though on close inspection the spotted flowers are quite pretty. It grows best in a sandy, fast-draining soil. Overly rich soil causes it to be floppy and reduces flowering. Bergamot prefers full sun but will also do well in partial shade.

This plant was dubbed bergamot by early settlers who found its citrusy scent and taste reminiscent of old-world bergamot (an extract from a tropical tree, actually), which is used to flavor Earl Grey tea. An infusion of the leaves makes a gentle, soothing tea—add a little orange rind to bring out the natural flavor.

An oil pressed from bergamot leaves contains thymol, a substance known to help heal fungal infections when applied topically. Internal use of the oil can be dangerous, however, provoking vomiting and diarrhea. Nowadays, thymol is produced synthetically. And herb gardeners needn't fret—tea made from bergamot leaves will not have a high concentration of the oil.

Betony

Stachys officinalis

HEIGHT/WIDTH: 2'–3' × 1' (60–90cm × 30cm)

FLOWERS/BLOOM TIME: red-purple/mid- to late summer

ZONES: 4–9

RECOMMENDED USES: medicinal, culinary

Betony

Without a doubt one of the prettiest herbs you can grow, betony is related to lamb's ears (*Stachys byzantina*), the popular perennial-garden stalwart. Like that plant, betony forms a rosette of downy leaves and features rosy purple flower spikes in the latter part of the summer, but its foliage is deep green and toothed rather than silvery gray and smooth-edged. The combination of dark foliage and rich-colored blossoms on this branching plant is irresistible. It may steal the show in your herb garden, and can certainly be added to a traditional flower border or even used as a tall edging, perhaps at the feet of some rose bushes. It will toler-ate partial shade, but it must have fertile yet not overrich, well-drained soil—it is not a drought-tolerant plant.

Betony has enjoyed a long and colorful reputation as a healing herb. It has been credited with easing everything from headaches to hearing difficulties to problems with internal organs—and with warding off evil spirits. But its most established and reliable use, thanks to the tannin content of its dried leaves, is simply as a soothing tea to relieve sore throats or diarrhea. The tea can also be drunk just for pleasure; it has a sweet, minty flavor.

Bistort

Polygonum bistorta

HEIGHT/WIDTH: 2'–3' × 1' (60–90cm × 30cm)

FLOWERS/BLOOM TIME: pink spikes/late spring to
summer

ZONES: 4–9

RECOMMENDED USES: culinary, medicinal

Bistort

You may start out valuing this unsung plant for its early and long-lasting blooms; the dense spikes are bright pink, especially when grown in full sun, in damp to average soil. However, you will also appreciate it throughout the summer for its handsome form and easy care. The leaves are a soft shade of blue-green and have a slightly wrinkled texture. They're edible, and taste best when eaten young. Toss a few in a salad with your first lettuce harvest.

But the plant's main attraction to herbalists over the years has been its root—more properly its chubby, creeping, reddish rhizome. Its astringent juice was used in the tanning of leather for a long time, until modern chemicals upstaged it. Herbalists also dried and powdered it for a sharp-flavored tea used in treating internal bleeding, gastronomic distress, and even diabetes. When the powder was moistened and pressed on cuts and wounds, it helped stop the bleeding and promoted faster healing. None of these applications has received the blessing of modern medicine, and you may not want to go to all the trouble, but you will always enjoy the plant as a handsome ornamental addition to your garden.

Black cumin

Nigella sativa

HEIGHT/WIDTH: 12″–18″ × 8″–12″ (30–45cm × 20-30cm)

FLOWERS/BLOOM TIME: light blue/midsummer

ZONES: all zones (annual)

RECOMMENDED USES: culinary

Black cumin

Not related to true cumin (*Cuminum cyminum*), this airy plant is much easier to grow. It can be direct-sown in light soil in full sun. You may be familiar with its cousin, love-in-a-mist (*Nigella damascena*), which has the same distinctive-looking flowers and is increasingly popular with gardeners who seek out unusual annuals. Black cumin's flowers are a lighter color, sometimes nearly white—and by season's end, they develop inflated seedpods that contain pungent and edible seeds.

To harvest the seeds, wait until late summer or early autumn, when the half-inch (12mm), horned seedpods turn brown and dry. Mash them open, and you'll discover several dozen black triangular seeds. Sift out the chaff and store the seeds in a cool, dry place. They have a wonderful, earthy flavor, not quite as powerful as regular cumin. Try them whole in baked goods, especially breads and rolls, or grind them into a powder and add them to soups, stews, or African and Mexican casseroles.

Bloodroot

Sanguinaria canadensis

HEIGHT/WIDTH: 6″–14″ × 6″–8″ (15–35cm × 15–20cm)

FLOWERS/BLOOM TIME: white/spring

ZONES: 3–8

RECOMMENDED USES: dye, medicinal

Bloodroot

This native North American wildflower was used by indigenous people before European settlers arrived in this country. It is still a familiar sight in early spring in wooded areas of the Northeast, where it thrives in rich, moist, acidic soil. The deeply lobed, heart-shaped leaves are very distinctive, and the creamy white blossoms are beautiful. Rock gardeners and connoisseurs of perennials often grow the showier, double-flowered variety 'Multiplex'.

Perhaps bloodroot's most notable use is as a dye. The juicy sap, which bleeds from a clipped stem or nicked root, is orange-red and colors skin and fabric easily. Be forewarned that the fixing action of a "mordant" additive will alter the color away from orange and more toward rust or pink, depending on what you use.

Bloodroot sap's therapeutic uses are legion, but are not to be attempted at home, as the wrong dose may be toxic. The sap is a source of an alkaloid called (not surprisingly) sanguinarine, which is said to be a potent stimulant and expectorant. Some modern research has linked it to the successful treatment of certain cancers. Consult a doctor for more information if you're interested.

Borage

Borago officinalis

HEIGHT/WIDTH: 2'–3' × 1'–2' (60–90cm × 30–60cm)

FLOWERS/BLOOM TIME: blue/summer

ZONES: all zones (annual)

RECOMMENDED USES: medicinal, culinary

Borage

Borage is an eager grower, blooms heavily, and brings charm and good looks to your summer garden. The slightly furry, gray-green leaves are quickly joined by the flowers, which appear in lush, drooping clusters. Individual flowers are star-shaped and anywhere from sky blue to vivid purple. Grow the plant in full sun in moist but well-drained soil, and place it where it will have room to sprawl and where you can appreciate the flowers from the side or below—a slope or upper terrace would be perfect. You'll notice that borage attracts lots of bees, so that may also be a consideration in placement.

The entire borage plant is edible, and has a flavor that has been compared to cucumbers, making it a nice addition to fresh salads, cold soups, or iced summer beverages. The flowers are a popular choice for candying because they are both safe and pretty.

Borage is credited with many medicinal uses, including relief for bronchitis, fever, and gastronomical woes, as well as being a diuretic. The seeds contain a compound found to be useful in treating premenstrual distress. But for the average gardener, the most practical medical use is to soothe cuts or bug bites with a cooling poultice of borage leaves.

Bouncing bet

Saponaria officinalis

HEIGHT/WIDTH: 1′–2′ × 1′–2′ (30–60cm × 30–60cm)

FLOWERS/BLOOM TIME: pink-white/mid- to late summer

ZONES: 3–8

RECOMMENDED USES: cosmetic

Bouncing bet

When does a roadside "weed" become an herb? When the gardener discovers that it is not only easy to grow, but has intriguing virtues. Such is the case with bouncing bet, a perky little plant with delicate-looking flowers. It is related to garden dianthus and carnations, and shares with them a delicious, sweet scent with a hint of cloves. Grow bouncing bet in almost any soil, as long as it is well-drained, in full sun or partial shade. It will self-sow, so plant it where you'd like it to naturalize. If you don't want bouncing bet to spread, make certain to pick the flowers before they go to seed.

The sap of this plant is naturally soapy. This quality is most easily extracted by simmering fresh stems and leaves in a pot of rainwater, well water, or bottled water (not chemically treated tap water) for about half an hour. The mild, fragrant lather that results can be used to gently wash and revitalize delicate fabrics such as lace, old linen, wool, or kid gloves. It can also be used to wash the hands and face and soothe acne, eczema, and itchy rashes like poison oak and ivy. Warning: bouncing bet should never be ingested. Not only is its soapy flavor unpleasant, it is a strong purgative and can be dangerous.

Burnet

Poterium sanguisorba

HEIGHT/WIDTH: 8″–30″ × 12″ (20–75cm × 30cm)

FLOWERS/BLOOM TIME: tiny pink and green balls/ summer

ZONES: 4–9

RECOMMENDED USES: culinary

Burnet

The botanical name of this ancient herb reveals its long-popular use: *poterium*, from the Greek, refers to a drinking cup. Sprigs are used to garnish glasses of wine and will also bring a refreshing touch to iced teas and punches. Fresh, young leaves have a cool, cucumberlike taste. Unfortunately, when dried, they lose their flavor, so this is a plant to pick and use on the spot. Its most popular use is as a salad green (it also goes by the name salad burnet), but creative cooks mince it and add it to coleslaw, dips, herb butters, and cold summer soups.

The plant itself has a delicate, almost frail appearance that looks sweet among lacy herbs such as the silvery artemisias. But it gets overwhelmed if interplanted with huskier plants. It begins as a low clump and sends up stalks lined with rounded leaflets. Though you'll have to look closely to appreciate the detail, burnet's tiny flowers are globe-shaped and lime green with tiny, rosy pink pistils and stamens spraying out at all angles. Remove them regularly if you want a continuous harvest of fresh new leaves.

Burnet is a very hardy plant, requires little attention from the gardener, and will self-seed over the years. It prospers in full sun or light shade. Its only quirk is a preference for dryish soil that is on the sweet (alkaline) side; it does not prosper in damp or highly acidic soils.

Calamint

Calamintha grandiflora

HEIGHT/WIDTH: 12"–14" × 8" (30–35cm × 20cm)

FLOWERS/BLOOM TIME: pink/mid- to late summer

ZONES: 5–9

RECOMMENDED USES: culinary, medicinal, craft

Calamint

As you might guess from the name, this herb is a mint relative. The scent of the leaves has been likened to camphor and, more poetically, tangerine-mint. The leaves are toothed and blue-green and, thanks to the plant's creeping rootstock, stay fairly low to the ground. The dense whorls of flowers rise above this mound and are anywhere from lilac to bright pink.

A plant this attractive and manageable is a good citizen in a carefully laid-out herb garden, but could also be used as a groundcover or tucked into a rock garden. You might prefer the variegated version, which grows a little more compactly and features white-speckled foliage.

Dried calamint leaves make an invigorating hot or iced tea that reminds one of peppermint tea. And because their scent is persistent, they make a nice addition to potpourri. Fresh leaves have been touted as a soothing dressing for bruises.

Calendula

Calendula officinalis

HEIGHT/WIDTH: 1′–2′ × 1′–2′ (30–60cm × 30–60cm)

FLOWERS/BLOOM TIME: yellow to orange/summer

ZONES: all zones (annual)

RECOMMENDED USES: culinary, medicinal, cosmetic, dye

Calendula

It's hard to imagine a more versatile, useful plant than calendula. A native of southern and central Europe that has gained use practically worldwide, it's been in cultivation for centuries. The cheerful yellow to orange flowers appear early and repeatedly. The flower heads are up to 4 inches (10cm) across, and there are now a number of improved varieties with larger, denser (even double) heads, taller stems, and bright, consistent colors. All calendula needs is full sun and average, well-drained soil.

The flowers are the main attraction for herbal uses. Picked fresh, the petals are a pretty, if not particularly flavorful, garnish for salads and soups (the flavor is subtly sweet). For drying, petals should be pulled loose and separated to dry on a screen; they'll retain their color well.

Calendula petals have been used as a substitute for the more expensive saffron in soups, rice dishes, and sauces. Boiled in water, they yield a bright yellow liquid that has been used as a dye. And a strong infusion made from the petals has been shown to kill some bacteria and fungi, which validates the plant's folk uses as a treatment for everything from cuts, bruises, and topical infections to chicken pox and measles. Calendula is gentle enough to use on babies or others with sensitive skin and can be found as an ingredient in soothing natural lotions and creams. People with light-colored hair can use calendula-based shampoos and rinses to bring out highlights.

Caper

Capparis spinosa

HEIGHT/WIDTH: 2'–3' × 2'–3' (60–90cm × 60–90cm)

FLOWERS/BLOOM TIME: white/early summer

ZONES: 7–10

RECOMMENDED USES: culinary

Caper

A rounded, shrubby plant, caper hails from rocky, dry Mediterranean hillsides. It can certainly be grown in any similar climate, as in the South or West, or anywhere else in a pot and overwintered in a greenhouse. As you might guess, it is quite heat and drought tolerant, though it should be watered regularly until well established.

The leaves are shiny and oval, and are borne on long, arching stems. They should be trimmed back a few inches every year just to keep the plant looking tidy. The small green buds develop into lovely but frail white blossoms 2 or 3 inches (5 or 7.5cm) across and centered with showy purple- or red-tipped stamens. The petals fall off within a day, but the plant keeps pumping out more flowers all summer.

Even if you are captivated by low-maintenance caper's beauty, you should harvest the tasty, tender immature buds. Collect them when they reach the size of peas, and preserve them in a vinegar-based pickling mixture. They are wonderful with eggplant and tomato dishes, and add real zest to any number of Greek, Italian, or Spanish recipes. A small jar makes a novel gift for your favorite chef.

Caraway

Carum carvi

HEIGHT/WIDTH: 24″ × 6″–12″ (60cm × 15–30cm)

FLOWERS/BLOOM TIME: white umbels/spring

ZONES: 4–8

RECOMMENDED USES: culinary, medicinal

Caraway

Savory caraway makes you wait for its seed harvest, but the plant is easy to grow and the homegrown seeds are so delicious, it's worth the delay. All it asks is full sun and fertile, well-drained soil. A biennial, caraway spends its first year establishing a strong root system and forming a short plant of rather feathery foliage. The following summer, it adds hollow stems topped with flat umbels of white flowers.

When the umbels start to turn brown late in their second summer, they are ready to be harvested. Clip them off and hang them upside down in a cool, dark place in a paper bag. The paper bag will catch the tiny crescent-shaped seeds as they fall. Dry the seeds thoroughly (a week or two) before storing them in a jar.

Caraway seeds have many, many uses, though their most popular modern use is as a nutty-licorice flavor ingredient in breads (especially rye and Irish soda bread), cookies, crackers, and apple pie. They're also a common ingredient in sauerkraut and other cabbage dishes (perhaps due to their reputation as a digestive aid), and may be added to meats—especially pork—to good effect. When possible, add them late in the recipe, as overcooked seeds tend to become bitter.

Cardamom

Elettaria cardamomum

HEIGHT/WIDTH: 6′–12′ × 2′–4′ (180–360cm × 60–120cm)

FLOWERS/BLOOM TIME: white to yellow/spring

ZONES: 9–10 (or grow as a houseplant in other zones)

RECOMMENDED USES: culinary, medicinal

Cardamom

Also known as "cinnamon palm," this shrubby plant is related to the showy ornamental gingers popular in some southern and Gulf Coast gardens. In more northern zones, it can be grown in a container and overwintered in a warm spot indoors or in a greenhouse. In any event, this native of the tropics must have plenty of moisture and partial shade in order to prosper. It has deep green, lance-shaped leaves about a foot (30cm) long. The small flowers appear in long racemes and are followed by the prized seedpods.

If you succeed in growing this difficult plant, you'll have a real treat with the seed harvest, as store-bought cardamom rapidly loses its scent and flavor. Each pod contains three sections, or cells, and small, fragrant, mahogany-colored seeds lurk inside. Do not split open the pods until just before you are ready to use them. A couple of seeds (bruise them first) make a splendid, exotically spicy addition to mulled wine or cider, and add enchanting aroma and taste to an ordinary pot of coffee. You can chew on a few for a breath freshener and to alleviate indigestion. Ground cardamom is also used in breads, cakes, and pastries. It is a popular ingredient in many East Indian, Arabic, African, and Scandinavian recipes.

Catnip

Nepeta cataria

HEIGHT/WIDTH: 1′–3′ × 1′–2′ (30–90cm × 30–60cm)

FLOWERS/BLOOM TIME: white with lavender/mid- to late summer

ZONES: 3–10

RECOMMENDED USES: medicinal

Catnip

Even if you're the sort of gardener who believes in sharing your garden with wildlife, your generosity may still be tested when you find this handsome herb constantly flattened by enthusiastic felines. On the other hand, perhaps you feel they should have some fun, too! Scientists who've studied this famous attraction have found that catnip's irresistible active ingredient is a volatile chemical called nepetalactone. Cats crush, bite, and chew the plant not to ingest it but to release the scent into the air. Depending on the particular plant, the dose, and the cat, it acts as a sedative or an aphrodisiac. As for its effects on humans, catnip has been shown to have no significant psychoactive properties except perhaps as a digestive aid and a mild sedative when the dried leaves are made into a rather tasty hot tea.

Catnip plants grow quickly and thickly, with soft green leaves that are soon joined by airy spires of white to lavender flowers. They must have well-drained soil, and you shouldn't pamper them too much or they'll spread rampantly, like any mint. Either full sun or partial shade will do. A more compact relative that also seems to be less of a cat magnet is *Nepeta mussinii* 'Blue Wonder'.

Chamomile

Chamaemelum nobile

HEIGHT/WIDTH: 3″–9″ × 12″ (7.5–22.5cm × 30cm)

FLOWERS/BLOOM TIME: tiny daisies/summer

ZONES: 3–9

RECOMMENDED USES: culinary, medicinal, cosmetic

Chamomile

This gentle herb is beloved for its sweet apple scent. It's actually a rather tough, sprawling, winter-hardy little groundcover. In fact, some gardeners like to slip it between paving stones on a path or terrace, where it will take foot traffic well and reward passersby with its enchanting aroma. (In medieval times, it was used as a strewing herb and an air freshener.) Of course, if you'd prefer, you can grow chamomile in the more congenial conditions of the garden proper, where it does best in light, dry soil. You can also grow it in a pot or window box. Full sun is best.

Chamomile's most famous use is as a soothing herbal tea. This may be brewed from the dried flowers—more properly the yellow centers, as the white "petals," or ray flowers, tend to fall off. It is credited with soothing indigestion, menstrual cramps, insomnia, and jangled nerves. (No wonder Peter Rabbit's mother gave him a cupful after his ordeal in Farmer McGregor's garden.) It is also added to hand and face lotions. As an ingredient in shampoo, it brings out blond highlights.

Chervil

Anthriscus cerefolium

HEIGHT/WIDTH: 24″ × 8″–12″ (60cm × 20–30cm)

FLOWERS/BLOOM TIME: tiny white umbels/summer

ZONES: all zones (annual)

RECOMMENDED USES: culinary

Chervil

You may never go back to parsley once you've tried the fresh yet delicate, almost aniselike, flavor of chervil, its close relative. This lovely herb looks a bit like parsley, with plenty of cut and divided leaves and leaflets, though it has a lacier, more graceful profile and it doesn't grow as wide or tall. The flowers are small white umbels that wave gently above the foliage. At season's end, chervil turns pale pink and then increasingly red, adding a nice touch of autumn color to the herb garden. It often self-sows, so you may have more plants to enjoy next year. Chervil thrives in partial shade and moist soil.

To use tasty chervil to its full potential, harvest young leaves and, if you wish, young stems. Chop them up and add generous handfuls to everything from salads to soups and sauces, or try them in egg dishes and casseroles. Wait to add chervil until late in the recipe, or the leaves will lose their flavor and texture. Small, fresh-cut sprigs also make a nice garnish. Dried chervil is not nearly as flavorful as fresh, but it is a component of fines herbes. This famous French cooking blend also includes dried parsley, thyme, and tarragon—again, this should be added to a recipe in the last few minutes for maximum effect.

Chia

Salvia columbariae

HEIGHT/WIDTH: 8"–18" × 6"–12" (20–45cm × 15–30cm)

FLOWERS/BLOOM TIME: blue/summer

ZONES: 8–10

RECOMMENDED USES: culinary, craft

Chia

Chia is a pretty, smallish sage from the chaparral and desert areas of the West, and as such grows best in hot, dry settings and requires well-drained soil. (And yes, it's the plant used for "chia pets.") Downy, wrinkled, dark green leaves appear first in a basal rosette, and line the erect stems at intervals, so the plant's profile is more airy than some of its relatives. The blue flowers with purple bracts stand out well in the herb garden. Wonderfully fragrant, chia can be dried and added to potpourri, and can also be used in the kitchen as you would other sages (in soups, roasted poultry and meat, stuffing, and sausage, for example).

Unlike other sages, chia has long been prized for its edible seeds. Native American tribes nibbled on them raw, and roasted and sprinkled them on many dishes. They also ground the seeds and used the flour in baking, and added it to a refreshing beverage. Those who fancy sprouts in their salads and sandwiches have discovered that chia sprouts have a pleasant, delicate flavor. (Make your own sprouts by placing ripe seeds on a damp paper towel for a few days.) The word "chia" comes from the Mayan language and means "strengthening," but knowledge of the plant's healing properties seems to be lost to history.

Chicory

Cichorium intybus

HEIGHT/WIDTH: 3′–5′ × 1′ (90–150cm × 30cm)

FLOWERS/BLOOM TIME: blue/summer

ZONES: 4–9

RECOMMENDED USES: culinary

Chicory

Have you ever had a cup of real New Orleans roast coffee, the kind where you keep adding milk or cream but the brew seems to stay persistently dark and powerful? Chances are you were at the mercy of chicory-enhanced coffee. Chicory is supposed to mellow coffee's flavor, and it does not contain any caffeine. But it does feature sedative, laxative, and diuretic properties. Thus chicory, while nontoxic, is not entirely innocuous.

The dark, gnarly, bittersweet root is harvested in autumn. Dried and ground, it looks a lot like coffee. In fact, in the nineteenth century, consumers complained that they were being tricked by unscrupulous merchants who sold ground chicory root as coffee or at least cut their coffee blends with it. The uproar led to the first pure-food labeling legislation.

The plant itself is a familiar roadside weed, originally from Europe but now widespread in North America. So, not surprisingly, it is an undemanding garden plant, and seems to want nothing more than a sunny spot. The jaunty blue flowers are prolific and pretty, but you'll notice that they are open only in the mornings. They close up shop by afternoon, even on sunny days.

Chives

Allium schoenoprasum

HEIGHT/WIDTH: 12″–18″ × 6″–8″ (30–45cm × 15–20cm)

FLOWERS/BLOOM TIME: bluish pink to lavender/early summer

ZONES: 3–9

RECOMMENDED USES: culinary, craft

Chives

Easy to grow and more attractive than other members of the onion and garlic family, cheery chives are a wonderful addition to any garden. The smallish, globe-shaped flowers are lovely, and the clump-forming plant doesn't grow to towering heights or flop over constantly. Some people even add chives to the flower border (beware of self-sowing, however). A lot of companion-planting lore is attached to chives, too: they're said to prevent blackspot on roses, mildew on cucumbers and squashes, scab on apples, and so on.

Chives are unique because they don't have a long natural dormant period. So if you live in a mild climate, you'll be harvesting year-round. In cold-winter areas, consider digging up some plants in late summer, potting them, and letting them die down outdoors through a frost or two. Then bring the pots inside to the kitchen windowsill, where they'll resprout. The harvest will be especially welcome on frosty nights when you're serving mashed potatoes with dinner.

The grassy, hollow leaves are, of course, a popular addition to salads, soups, and spreads. What you may not know is that the flowers are also edible and can make a pretty contribution to the same dishes. Dried-flower arrangers like the flowers because they keep their shape and color well and don't shatter.

Clary

Salvia sclarea

HEIGHT/WIDTH: 3′–5′ × 2′–3′ (90–150cm × 60–90cm)

FLOWERS/BLOOM TIME: white to lavender/summer

ZONES: 6–9

RECOMMENDED USES: medicinal, cosmetic, culinary

Clary

Apparently "clary" is a shortened version of this sage's earlier name, "clear eye," which it earned from its reputation as an eyewash. A boiled seed produced a thick mucilaginous gel that was applied to the irritated eye. The theory behind this rather farfetched process was that the offending foreign particle(s) would adhere to the gel; when everything was removed from the eye, clear sight would be restored.

It is also known as muscatel sage in Europe, where a liquid made from steeping the leaves along with some elder flowers was added to Rhine wines, mimicking the sweet flavor of muscadine grapes. Beer brewers have reportedly used clary sage in the absence of hops.

Modern gardeners in mild climates are most apt to grow this plant for its strong, appealing fragrance. More like balsam than mint, the scent is a terrific additive for homegrown cosmetics (bath mixtures, soap, lotion, etc.). A tea brewed from the dried leaves is said to settle an upset stomach. You can also use the dried leaves in any recipe that would be enhanced by other sages.

One caveat: clary is a biennial, and won't flower until its second season. The flower-and-bract colors vary quite a bit, too, from near-white to pink to lavender. Grow it in average to dry soil in full sun.

Comfrey

Symphytum officinale

HEIGHT/WIDTH: 2'–3' × 2'–3' (60–90cm × 60–90cm)

FLOWERS/BLOOM TIME: pink to blue/summer

ZONES: 5–9

RECOMMENDED USES: medicinal (with care), cosmetic

Comfrey

Comfrey has been cultivated and prized for many uses over the centuries, though its reputation has lost some of its luster under the scrutiny of modern science. The leaves contain calcium, phosphorus, potassium, and vitamins A, B_{12} (quite rare in plants), and C. Such a bounty made them a popular part of the vegetarian diet for many years, whether chopped fresh into salads and other dishes or cooked like spinach.

In recent years, however, several studies have called comfrey's safety into question, and until scientists sort it all out, we are advised not to ingest it. Apparently, lab rats fed on a diet that includes comfrey leaves quickly develop liver cancer, probably due to the presence of harmful alkaloids.

Comfrey is also credited with healing abilities when applied topically, and these have not been called into doubt. In fact, the leaves and the sticky root have been shown to contain soothing allantoin, a protein that helps regenerate damaged tissue. A poultice of the leaves, or a store-bought cream containing allantoin, can ease everything from athlete's foot to burns to sores. In years past, comfrey was also prescribed for broken bones and open wounds.

As a garden plant, this herb is not for the fainthearted. It gets rather large and rangy, and its big taproot makes it difficult to move once established (plus, root fragments, given half a chance, generate new plants). The dark green, prickly leaves grow long and thick. The flowers, borne in nodding bell-like clusters, are pink and blue. Plant comfrey toward the back of your herb garden or anywhere it can spread out, in moist, fertile soil and full sun or light shade.

Coneflower

Echinacea spp.

HEIGHT/WIDTH: 1'–3' × 1–2' (30–90cm × 30–60cm)

FLOWERS/BLOOM TIME: purple daisies/summer

ZONES: 3–9

RECOMMENDED USES: medicinal

Purple coneflower

Native to North America, these handsome plants provided the indigenous people with many remedies, and some of these uses prevail to this day. You won't find them listed on the labels of products in regular drugstores, mainly because newer and apparently more effective substitutes exist. But coneflower's popularity continues unabated on the shelf in health-food stores. It is nontoxic.

Coneflower's useful part is the spindly brown root of mature plants. The Plains Indians sucked on it to treat mumps, measles, smallpox, venereal diseases, and even tumors. They also valued it for easing sore throats and toothaches. And it helped heal topical problems such as sores, wounds, insect bites, snake bites, and infections. Modern clinical studies have shown that this wide range was justified; the plant is capable of activating the body's immune system and has antiviral and antibacterial properties. For this reason, some people take coneflower tablets or drink the tea as a preventive.

Echinacea angustifolia is not as tall or showy as the more commonly grown *E. purpurea* (purple coneflower) but it is certainly attractive in its own right and perhaps better suited to today's smaller gardens. Both are very hardy perennial plants and thrive in most soils, so long as the drainage is good. They're also fairly drought tolerant. Harvest and dry the root only after the plant is three or four years old; make your move in autumn, when the plants are going dormant.

Coriander

Coriandrum sativum

HEIGHT/WIDTH: 12″–36″ × 8″–12″ (30–90cm × 20–30cm)

FLOWERS/BLOOM TIME: pink/summer

ZONES: all zones (annual)

RECOMMENDED USES: culinary, medicinal

Coriander

Although coriander can be tricky to grow, this herb rewards the diligent gardener with its many uses. An annual, it's best sown directly into the garden after the last frost. It requires well-drained soil and cannot tolerate "wet feet." Coriander grows quickly, sending up frail, slender stalks topped with tiny umbels of pinkish flowers. Until it is well established, keep the bed weeded and mulched.

Harvest the savory, lemony leaves—known as cilantro or Chinese parsley—early. You want to pick the young leaves, which look very much like parsley. Older leaves are as feathery as dill and not nearly as appealing. It is also important to harvest relatively quickly because the plant tends to go to seed early. Successive sowings will assure you a continuous harvest. Fresh-chopped leaves are a common ingredient in Asian recipes and are also used in Mexican, North African, and Caribbean dishes and sauces. Note that dried leaves are virtually flavorless.

Some cooks harvest the small, spicy seeds. Proper timing is key: use the seeds too early, and they have a distinctly unpleasant odor; too late, and they have scattered themselves on the ground. Catch the seeds as they're turning brown, and dry them further before storing. They'll become more aromatic with age. Use them whole or ground in curries, soups, cooked vegetable dishes, and fruit breads and cakes. You may also nibble on a few, or make a tea, to treat an upset stomach.

Costmary

Tanacetum (Chrysanthemum) balsamita

HEIGHT/WIDTH: 1′–3′ × 1′–2′ (30–90cm × 30–60cm)

FLOWERS/BLOOM TIME: tiny daisies/summer

ZONES: 4–9

RECOMMENDED USES: culinary, craft

Costmary

Despite the fact that it is not a very striking plant, costmary has a colorful history. The aromatic leaves, smelling of mint to some noses, balsam to others, served many uses. They were added to ale to help preserve it and to contribute a minty bitter flavor (hence the plant's other common name, alecost), used as a strewing herb, and steeped in water to make a mild infusion for washing and scenting fine linens. Nowadays, whole or chopped leaves may enhance cool summer drinks such as iced tea and lemonade. The flowers, which appear in the latter part of the summer, are very small yellow daisies.

Costmary sprigs were often pressed between the pages of the family Bible, a tradition that is traced back to the early Puritans. But they were more than a mere bookmark. Herbalists are quick to point out that costmary was also a practical choice—apparently, a drowsy parishioner could revive himself by sniffing or chewing on the bookmark if need be. Dried and crumbled leaves, flowers, and stems also make nice sachets.

Grow this herb in full sun in well-drained soil. Be forewarned that it can get leggy (so harvest leaves or sprigs regularly) and it will spread quickly via its creeping rootstock.

Cumin

Cuminum cyminum

HEIGHT/WIDTH: *6″–12″ × 3″–6″ (15-30cm × 7.5–15cm)*

FLOWERS/BLOOM TIME: white to pink/summer

ZONES: all zones (annual)

RECOMMENDED USES: culinary

Cumin

If you love to cook, growing cumin may be on your wish list. Unfortunately, it is not always an easy project. For one, the plants are small and vulnerable. They never get very large or wide, and their leaves are thin and threadlike. They sulk in soil that is too wet, die out in soil that is too dry, and languish in settings that are exposed to too much sun or wind. The good news is that some gardeners have successfully conquered these problems by growing cumin plants in small pots, placing them in a sheltered spot, and keeping a constant eye on them.

To harvest those wonderfully earthy, spicy seeds, you'll also need a long growing season—up to four months—or a good head start indoors. Like other umbel-forming herbs, you want to wait until the flower heads begin to turn brown before harvesting them. In a cool, dry place, dry them upside down in a brown paper bag, or tug off the seeds and lay them on a sheet. Later, store the precious harvest, whole or ground, in an airtight jar. Add to curries and chili powder or directly to soups, stews, or casseroles. Cumin is often found in Middle Eastern, Indian, and Mexican recipes.

Dame's rocket

Hesperis matronalis

HEIGHT/WIDTH: 1′–3′ × 1′–2′ (30–90cm × 30–60cm)

FLOWERS/BLOOM TIME: pink, purple, or white/summer

ZONES: 4–8

RECOMMENDED USES: culinary, craft

Dame's rocket

Looking a bit like a wild version of garden phlox (although the two are not related), dame's rocket is a delightful plant. The color varies from creamy white to softest pink to nearly magenta to purple, and the flowers are sweetly clove-scented, making them a lovely choice for summer bouquets. If you leave them be in the garden, you'll notice that their fragrance is especially strong in the evening, when they attract pollinating moths. The common name comes from the tradition of using the blooms to scent ladies' chambers.

Please note, however, that this plant is biennial, so you'll have to wait to enjoy the bounty in its second season.

Thereafter, though, dame's rocket will self-sow readily, and you'll never be without.

The spear-shaped, toothed leaves are a dark mint green, and have been used in salads. They have a sharp, tangy flavor like some of their close relatives in the mustard (arugula) family. The youngest ones are the most tender and tasty. The flowers are also edible; charm your guests by sprinkling them in a salad, atop a dip, or as a garnish for a cold soup or dessert. Dried, they retain their color and scent fairly well, so you may enjoy adding them to potpourris.

Dill

Anethum graveolens

HEIGHT/WIDTH: 2′–5′ × 2′ (60–150cm × 60cm)

FLOWERS/BLOOM TIME: yellow umbels/summer

ZONES: all zones (annual)

RECOMMENDED USES: culinary

Dill

As a culinary herb with edible leaves as well as edible seeds, lovely dill is hard to beat. It grows easily and eagerly, rewards with a delicious harvest, and self-sows. All it asks for is regular watering; it prospers in rich, well-drained soil, but will still produce in less-than-ideal conditions. About the only criticism gardeners ever have of it is that the plant is a rangy, sometimes floppy grower. However, that problem can be avoided if you grow one of the newer, more compact cultivated varieties. The best one is 18-inch (45cm) -high 'Fern Leaf', which won All-America Selections honors in 1992. Another worthy dwarf variety is 'Dukat' ('Tetra').

The best time to harvest the leaves is early in the morning, when they are full of moisture. Use them promptly for maximum flavor—in salads, in seafood and chicken dishes, and in soups of all kinds. You may freeze any excess by rolling sprigs in plastic wrap.

If you want to harvest aromatic dill seeds, read seed packet or catalog descriptions carefully. A "slow-bolting" dill may give you plenty of luscious leaves but resist going to seed. To harvest, just hang a browning flower head over a sheet or cloth. Whole or ground, the seeds make a tasty addition to apple pie, herb butter, breads, cookies, and cakes. And of course, where would pickles be without dill seeds? (Some home canners also tuck in a few immature flower heads.) By the way, dill seeds are rich in mineral salts, so people on salt-free diets may want to try them.

Dittany of Crete

Origanum dictamnus

HEIGHT/WIDTH: $12'' \times 8''$–$12''$ ($30cm \times 20$–$30cm$)

FLOWERS/BLOOM TIME: pink with purple bracts/
summer

ZONES: 8–10 (elsewhere, grow in pots)

RECOMMENDED USES: medicinal

Dittany of Crete

Something of a novelty among herb fanciers, Dittany of Crete is related to the familiar oregano. As its name suggests, this small, shrubby, compact plant originally hails from Greece. As such, it is not a hardy plant, and must have protection from freezing. It is also a drought-tolerant sun lover and, in mild climates, makes a nice edging or rock-garden plant. In most of North America, however, it is grown in a hanging basket or in a pot on a windowsill.

Dittany of Crete has beautiful, thick, rounded, furry silver leaves that are crowned in summer with pretty blossoms of pink with darker, purple bracts. These are fatter than regular oregano flowers, and remind some people of hops blossoms. Collected and dried, they've been used to make a mild-flavored digestive tea. In centuries past, the plant was also reputed to have remarkable wound-healing abilities, but the methods have been lost to history.

Epazote

Chenopodium ambrosioides

HEIGHT/WIDTH: 2′–4′ × 1′–2′ (60–120cm × 30–60cm)

FLOWERS/BLOOM TIME: tiny, green/summer

ZONES: 5–10

RECOMMENDED USES: culinary

Epazote

Too often dismissed as a roadside weed, epazote is currently enjoying renewed interest thanks to the popularity of authentic Mexican cooking. Epazote is related to the valuable Andean grain plant quinoa (*C. quinoa*) and the spinach-like lambs' quarters (*C. album*), but is valued more for its ability to reduce flatulence than for any spectacular nutritional benefits.

The edible part of this plant is the leaves, and the young, smaller ones are best for cooking. They have a wild, powerful aroma that, while not offensive, takes some getting used to. Deeply cut or toothed, up to 5 inches (12.5cm) long, epazote leaves may be minced and added fresh to soups and stews, particularly ones that contain beans. It is also found in green mole and pipián sauces, where it contributes to the green color as well.

Grow this herb in full sun and well-drained soil. Beware, though: epazote is an enthusiastic grower and self-seeder, and can take over large areas in short order. You might be better off growing a few plants in pots.

Fennel

Foeniculum vulgare

HEIGHT/WIDTH: 3'–5' × 2'–4' (90–150cm × 60–120cm)

FLOWERS/BLOOM TIME: large yellow umbels/mid- to
late summer

ZONES: 6–9

RECOMMENDED USES: culinary, dye, cosmetic

Fennel

This big, bold herb radiates a sweet, warm licorice smell that's a bit more nutty than that of anise. In average but well-drained soil, it can soar up to 5 feet (1.5m) tall in a single season, topped with broad yellow umbels of flowers. You may wish to seek out the alternative variety known as bronze fennel, which is similar in every way except coloring. The contrast of its bronze stems and tinted foliage with the golden flower heads is a beautiful sight.

Fennel doubles as a vegetable and a spice. The sweet-flavored stalks, which resemble celery stalks, are tasty to nibble on raw, and can be diced into soups and salads or served steamed. The curved, greenish brown seeds are also prized. Watch the plant carefully late in the season and clip off the flower heads the moment you spot them going brown (turning ripe). Otherwise, even a slight breeze will spill your eagerly awaited harvest—and then you'll have more fennel plants in your garden in the coming years than you ever bargained for! Pop the harvested head in a paper bag, wait a week or two, and then collect your bounty and store it in an airtight jar. Use the seeds in bread baking, fish dishes, homemade sausages, and tomato-based sauces.

Fennel tea is a pleasant breath freshener and also enjoys a reputation as a diuretic (high doses can overstimulate the nervous system and should be avoided). The flowers and leaves have been used to make yellow and brown dyes for wool. Fennel is also used to scent soap as well as in steam facials as a pore cleanser.

Fenugreek

Trigonella foenum-graecum

HEIGHT/WIDTH: 1′–2′ × 1′–2′ (30–60cm × 30–60cm)

FLOWERS/BLOOM TIME: white, pealike/summer

ZONES: all zones (annual)

RECOMMENDED USES: culinary, medicinal

Fenugreek

You have to wonder how fenugreek's wonderful culinary properties were discovered in the first place. The plant, a member of the pea family, is somewhat lax and rangy, and looks a lot like ordinary clover. Native to the Mediterranean, it remains popular in that area as a fodder and agricultural cover crop. The small white flowers are practically lost in all the herbage, and the brown seedpods that follow (about 6 inches [15cm] long) don't stand out much either.

Even after you harvest those seedpods and extract the oblong, honey-colored seeds within, you won't find them very appealing. They have little scent and a bitter taste, and must be roasted carefully to bring out the splendid, spicy, maplelike flavor coveted by cooks the world over. Once the seeds are dried and ground, their scent and flavor reach their full potential. Fenugreek is a common ingredient in Indian curries and chutneys as well as many North African dishes. It is also used in halvah, the Middle Eastern sweet treat.

Modern science has discovered or verified from folk remedies some amazing properties in fenugreek seed — everything from lowering blood sugar in diabetics and easing gastronomic woes to treating impotence in men and easing both nursing and menopausal problems in women.

Feverfew

Tanacetum (Chrysanthemum) parthenium

HEIGHT/WIDTH: 2'–3' × 2'–3' (60–90cm × 60–90cm)

FLOWERS/BLOOM TIME: small daisies/summer

ZONES: 5–9

RECOMMENDED USES: medicinal

Feverfew

This pretty plant has a lot going for it. Easy to grow in almost any soil, it flowers profusely, is rarely troubled by pests or diseases, and makes a fairly tidy appearance. For this reason, it is often incorporated into regular flower gardens, used as an edging plant, and tucked into charming window box schemes.

But some gardeners have noticed an odd quirk: bees avoid feverfew, perhaps because of its strong, bitter smell (most noticeable to humans when plant parts are touched or crushed). So if you have a vegetable garden or other plants in your garden that rely on bee pollination, you might want to think twice about planting feverfew. It also likes to self-sow, but you may consider that a virtue.

Feverfew gets its common name from its long-standing reputation as a fever reducer. It is no longer credited with this ability, but researchers have verified another valuable quality lurking in its leaves: it has anti-inflammatory properties similar to that of aspirin. It is now being touted as a relief or even cure for headaches, including debilitating migraines. You'll find over-the-counter feverfew preparations on the shelves of many health-food stores. Eating the leaves fresh out of your garden is not recommended without the supervision of a qualified doctor or herbalist. In any event, the sharp, bitter flavor may put you off.

Flax

Linum usitatissimum

HEIGHT/WIDTH: 2′–4′ × 1′–2′ (60–120cm × 30–60cm)

FLOWERS/BLOOM TIME: blue/summer

ZONES: all zones (annual)

RECOMMENDED USES: craft

Flax

True flax, the flax that has been used for centuries to make linen, is an annual plant, not to be confused with the similar but shorter perennial *L. perenne*, but it is just as easy to grow. Sow seeds directly into your garden after the soil has warmed up and danger of frost has passed. Note that the plant is shallow-rooted, so choose a spot where your seedlings won't be disturbed by hoeing or foot traffic.

In bloom, flax is a pretty sight. Clouds of delicate, soft blue, half-inch (12mm) flowers cover the plant. Individual flowers wither and drop their petals quickly, but are just as quickly replaced. However, it is the stems that are most valued. The fibers that can be woven into linen cloth are inside; extracting them involves soaking the plants in water, scraping off the outer stem, and combing out the fine but strong fibers. They are at their best (soft yet tough) when harvested after the plant has bloomed, just as the stalks begin to dry and turn yellow.

This plant is also known as linseed, and a yellowish oil extracted from the brown seeds was used in times past as a cough medicine and laxative. It is not used today because scientists have identified a number of toxic chemicals, particularly in the immature seeds. Overdoses can lead to hyperventilating and even paralysis. Linseed oil is an ingredient in printing ink, paint, and varnish.

Garlic

Allium sativum

HEIGHT/WIDTH: 2′ × 1′ (60cm × 30cm)

FLOWERS/BLOOM TIME: white/summer

ZONES: 3–9

RECOMMENDED USES: culinary, medicinal

Garlic

If you love garlic, you owe it to yourself to raise it in your garden. Not only is it easy to grow, but you'll discover that the flavor is richer and more pungent than anything you've ever bought in the store. Garlic plants don't take up a lot of space, so you can plant a whole bed of them or just tuck a few behind some of your other herb plants. They do best in full sun in soil that is reasonably fertile and drains well.

The secret to growing good garlic is planting ahead of time—the previous autumn. But don't plant too late in the season; get the little cloves in the ground a month or more before you expect the ground to freeze. (You can plant grocery-store cloves, but mail-order companies offer a wider range of choices.)

They'll start forming roots, and when spring comes, the plants will burst into vigorous growth. Encourage them with a dose of fertilizer, if you wish. Snap off the odd-looking flowerstalks so that the plant's energy will be directed toward root development (these stalks, and the "bulbils" they are topped with, are edible—try them in salads). Around midsummer, you'll notice growth slowing down. Reduce watering, wait for the leaves to wither, then harvest what should be big, fat, juicy bulbs with the leaves still attached. Air dry for a few weeks, then braid them or store in a cool, dry place (never in the refrigerator).

As for garlic's culinary uses, entire cookbooks are devoted to the subject. Its medicinal uses are also legendary, and many have been verified by modern science. It is an antiseptic, brings relief to cold symptoms, lowers blood pressure, and is more effective than penicillin against typhus!

Garlic chives

Allium tuberosum

HEIGHT/WIDTH: 2'–3' × 1'–2' (60–90cm × 30–60cm)

FLOWERS/BLOOM TIME: white/late summer

ZONES: 3–9

RECOMMENDED USES: culinary

Garlic chives

Unlike some of its garlicky, oniony relatives, garlic chives' flowers are sweetly fragrant—the scent has even been compared to that of a rose. Shaped like starry tufts, the creamy white flowers are also pretty. They're edible, and make a nice seasoning or striking garnish.

But the real reason to grow this plant is for its foliage. Long, flat, and thin, it resembles chives but is taller. The subtle, garliclike flavor makes it ideal for mincing into salads, soups, and savory dips. Other names for this plant—Chinese chives, Chinese leeks, Oriental garlic, gow choy, chung fa, and yuen sai—reveal its importance in Asian cuisine. It is a common ingredient in stir-fries.

This perky little plant is a perennial, plus it self-sows with abandon, so unless you want an ever-burgeoning harvest you'll have to keep an eye on it. Like garlic, it wants decently well drained soil and a spot in full sun. Clip flowerstalks before they go to seed, and pull out unwanted plants as they appear.

Geranium

Pelargonium spp.

HEIGHT/WIDTH: 6"–36" × 6"–36" (15–90cm × 15–90cm)

FLOWERS/BLOOM TIME: not generally grown for flowers

ZONES: 9–10 (elsewhere, grow in pots)

RECOMMENDED USES: culinary, craft

Geranium

If fragrance is your goal in growing herbs, you must have some scented geraniums in your collection. They resemble the familiar window box geraniums, but the flowers are not nearly as showy. The leaves, especially when brushed against, radiate scent—everything from apple (*P. odoratissimum*) to chocolate peppermint (a hybrid) to lemon (*P. crispum*) to true rose (*P. graveolens*). You'll also appreciate the great variation in leaf shapes and textures. Some are broad, some are lacy; some are velvety soft, and some are crisp and smooth. Color may also vary, from dark emerald green to lime green with splashes or touches of black, darker green, cream, or yellow.

The only drawback to scented geraniums is that they are tender plants. However, they are charming in pots and window boxes, and you can overwinter them indoors. If that's too much trouble, simply take cuttings from your favorites toward the end of the summer and start new plants. In any case, they should be grown in a good, well-drained potting mix and watered regularly. Warm temperatures and good air circulation keep them healthy.

All scented geraniums make nice additions to potpourris and sachets. For best results, snip off leaves in the morning of a dry, sunny day and lay them to dry flat in the shade. Fresh-picked rose-scented leaves are a popular addition to apple jelly (just lay a leaf or two on top before sealing the jar). They'll also contribute their soft, sweet scent to a canister of white sugar, enhancing all sorts of baked goodies.

Germander

Teucrium chamaedrys

HEIGHT/WIDTH: 6″–18″ × 12″–18″ (15–45cm × 30–45cm)

FLOWERS/BLOOM TIME: pink to purple/summer

ZONES: 5–9

RECOMMENDED USES: medicinal

Germander

Germander is a handsome, fast-growing, shrubby mint relative. Its most popular use is as an edging plant in designed herb gardens (knot gardens, mazes, etc.). Indeed, it has sometimes been referred to as "the poor man's boxwood." More winter-hardy than boxwood, gardeners in more northern limits would still be wise to mulch it for the winter, just in case. Like boxwood, it responds well to shaping and pruning, filling in gaps quickly with fresh new growth. The tiny, half-inch (12mm) green leaves are small, stiff, and scalloped. Plant germander in full sun, in average, well-drained soil. Keep plants lush with a good pruning each spring.

Germander flowers may not be welcome in your hedging or edging scheme and can be clipped off as they appear. But, like all mint-family flowers, they are rather pretty—borne on upright stems, they vary from pink to purple.

As for uses, germander's main claim to fame is as a treatment for gout. Tea brewed from its leaves was credited with curing the sixteenth-century German emperor Charles V of gout. Germander was also employed in soothing cold symptoms and jaundice and reducing fever. Nowadays, other herbs can do a better job of treating the same ills, but germander's ornamental grace and beauty continue to be valued.

Ginger

Zingiber officinale

HEIGHT/WIDTH: 2′–4′ × 1′–2′ (60–120cm × 30–60cm)

FLOWERS/BLOOM TIME: greenish spikes/summer

ZONES: 9–10 (elsewhere, grow as a houseplant)

RECOMMENDED USES: culinary, medicinal

Ginger

Ah, ginger—so pungent, so spicy, so warming. And although it is a tropical plant, many gardeners have had good luck raising it at home from ordinary grocery-store rhizomes. All it needs is an ample pot of fertile, well-drained soil and a warm, sheltered spot out of direct sunlight. It appreciates extra humidity, which is easily provided by setting the pot on a tray of water and pebbles and by misting it occasionally. It will produce long, lance-shaped leaves and occasionally a flower that resembles a tiny pineapple.

But of course it is the root you are after, and the good news is that you can harvest after a year or less. Freshly harvested, your homegrown ginger root will have several branches and be plump and juicy, ready to add to stir-fries and marinades. Or, let it dry out and grate it into all sorts of dishes, from meats to vegetables to baked goods. Dried chunks may be candied for a delicious snack eaten straight or added to cookies or cakes.

Ginger also offers useful medicinal benefits. It eases indigestion, morning sickness, and motion sickness, and it has been found to be a stimulant that promotes circulation and the absorption of other medications. Ginger liniments are used to relax sore muscles.

Goldenseal

Hydrastis canadensis

HEIGHT/WIDTH: 6"–12" × 6"–8" (15–30cm × 15–20cm)

FLOWERS/BLOOM TIME: greenish/spring

ZONES: 5–9

RECOMMENDED USES: medicinal, with caution; dye

Goldenseal

A native American wildflower, goldenseal (its yellowish root, to be exact) is credited with all sorts of healing properties. And while it has been shown that many of these claims are inaccurate and that certain uses are in fact dangerous, its great popularity hasn't waned. The result is that wild stands are rapidly disappearing and the price is going up, up, up. It seems only logical, then, to try to grow your own.

Unfortunately, it is not easy to grow. Goldenseal is a woodland plant and needs similar conditions in cultivation: filtered shade, humid air, and soil that is rich, moist, and light. Best raised from pieces of sprouted root, a mature, usable harvest may be several years away. The plant itself is attractive but not especially unusual-looking. The leaves are light green and deeply lobed, the stems are erect and fuzzy, and the flowers are small and inconspicuous.

The active ingredient in the root is an alkaloid called hydrastine. In large doses, it adversely affects the nervous system and may lead to severe vomiting, respiratory failure, convulsions, paralysis, and death. Also, it lingers in your system and accumulates, so current conventional wisdom counsels against taking goldenseal internally. Apparently safe topical uses include using it to treat conjunctivitis, herpes, and canker sores. But as with some other potentially harmful herbs, it is best to check with your doctor or a professional herbalist before you use it. The belief that it masks the positive results of urine tests for drug users has been debunked. Also, dyes can be made from infusing the roots.

Good King Henry

Chenopodium bonus-henricus

HEIGHT/WIDTH: 1'–3' × 1'–2' (30–90cm × 30–60cm)

FLOWERS/BLOOM TIME: yellow/summer

ZONES: 5–8

RECOMMENDED USES: culinary

Good King Henry

Who was "Good King Henry," and how did his name become attached to this leafy European herb? The plant was not named for England's Henry VIII, whose reputation is not especially good anyway. Rather, the name appears to come from a German folk tale about a virtuous goblin named Henry who helped women with their household chores (which, presumably, included harvesting greens from the garden) in exchange for a saucer of milk.

This compact-growing plant is a pleasant addition to any garden, and brings broad-leaved texture to an herb-garden scheme that might otherwise be dominated by lacy foliage. The leaves, which have a distinctive arrow shape,

are glossy and dark green. Eat them raw or cooked, alone or in salads, casseroles, and soups. Keep in mind that the younger leaves taste best, much like a mild, tangy version of spinach. Their iron content is even higher than that of spinach.

Good King Henry grows best in deep, rich soil, and can be slow to get established. Depending on how it does for you, you might be wise to let it grow for a year and begin harvesting in the second summer. In any event, keep it well watered so that the leaves are at their succulent best. Trimming off the imconspicuous yellow flower spikes will keep the plant in production.

Horehound

Marrubium vulgare

HEIGHT/WIDTH: 1'–2' (30–60cm) × 1'–2' (30–60cm)

FLOWERS/BLOOM TIME: white/mid- to late summer

ZONES: 4–9

RECOMMENDED USES: medicinal

Horehound

Justly famous as a sore-throat and cough remedy, horehound has been prized since the days of ancient Egypt and Greece. In fact, its common name is believed to have been derived from Horus, the Egyptian god of the sky and light. The "hound" part may have to do with the old belief that it cures the bite of a mad dog.

The plant has a wonderful, distinctively menthollike scent with a touch of woodsiness. An extract from the leaves is used to this day in throat lozenges, cough drops, cough syrups, and sometimes savory candies. Apparently the plant's high concentration of mucilage gets the credit, but it also contains soothing volatile compounds and even some vitamin C.

Horehound is a bushy, branching plant, and the stems and leaves are extremely woolly and soft. The color is light green, but thanks to its overall furriness, horehound sometimes looks almost white. The small white flowers, which make their debut in the second season, don't stand out much to our eyes but are a magnet for bees.

Grow horehound in full sun in well-drained soil (even sandy soil is okay). Harvest the leaves early in the day and immediately dice them into small pieces and seal in an airtight jar (dried leaves quickly lose their potency). Brew in a soothing tea or make your own lozenges by boiling them with sugar, then cooling and cutting into small chunks.

Horseradish

Armoracia rusticana

HEIGHT/WIDTH: 2'–3' × 1' (60–90cm × 30cm)

FLOWERS/BLOOM TIME: small, white/early summer

ZONES: 5–8

RECOMMENDED USES: culinary, medicinal

Horseradish

The fresh root of this otherwise undistinguished-looking plant has a powerful flavor, unrivaled in the herb and vegetable world. Grow your own, and you will enjoy it at its full potency. But before you plant, pick the site with care. Horseradish will conquer the area in which it is planted in short order and is practically impossible to eradicate. Consign it to an out-of-the-way spot, or put it in a wide but bottomless container. Or, grow it as some people grow potatoes—in mounds—or in its own raised bed. Once you've taken care of that problem, devote some effort to soil preparation. The best horseradish roots—as with any root crop—are grown in rich, well-drained soil that is well sifted (free of rocks and clumps) and weed-free.

Harvest in autumn, after the floppy, oblong leaves begin to yellow. Clean off the roots and store them in the refrigerator, where they'll keep for up to three months. (They may also be stored in dry sand in a cool basement or garage.) The sooner you eat them, the more pungent the flavor will be. Note that the flavor does not survive cooking. A popular use for horseradish is to mince it, add it to mayonnaise or mustard, and serve with roast beef. It's also good with baked or cold fish and in fish salads. You may want to grate it into vinegar or lemon juice, which keeps the flavor intact while preventing discoloration.

Although it isn't used much as a remedy anymore, in times past horseradish was valued as a digestive aid and, not surprisingly, a way to clear the sinuses.

Hummingbird sage

Salvia leucantha

HEIGHT/WIDTH: 3′–5′ × 3′–5′ (90–150cm × 90–150cm)

FLOWERS/BLOOM TIME: lavender/late summer to fall

ZONES: 7–10

RECOMMENDED USES: craft

Hummingbird sage

Also known as Mexican bush sage, this attractive dry-climate plant forms a dense, shrubby mound of rough-textured gray-green leaves. Late in the season, the leaves are joined by masses of spectacular flowers. Borne in velvety spikes up to 8 inches (20cm) long, these are lavender to dark purple and accented by white or purple protruding "tongues" (corollas). Crowds of bees, butterflies, and, of course, hummingbirds flock to them. They're wonderful in bouquets and also dry well, so they are a nice addition to dried arrangements, wreaths, and swags.

There are a few cultivated varieties of hummingbird sage. 'All Purple' has rich, two-tone purple flowers.

'Emerald' flowers are lavender-purple accented with white, plus the foliage is a darker green than the species. 'Emeralds 'n' Cream' has the same flowers as 'Emerald', but with lovely variegated foliage.

Gardeners in mild climates should have no trouble growing this plant. But even if you're north of its hardiness range, you may want to give it a try; it's a fast grower and can reach a substantial size and flower in just one season. In any event, be sure to give it a spot with plenty of sun and decent, well-drained soil. Don't overwater, or it may languish. You may fertilize lightly to encourage flowering.

Hyssop

Hyssopus officinalis

HEIGHT/WIDTH: 2′–3′ × 1′–2′ (60–90cm × 30–60cm)

FLOWERS/BLOOM TIME: blue to purple/summer

ZONES: 4–8

RECOMMENDED USES: medicinal, culinary

Hyssop

Related to both the mints and the sages, easy-going hyssop is a bit like each of them. Along with the characteristic square stems of mint, it also has the powerful scent you'd expect (almost too powerful for some tastes, and more camphorlike than mint-sweet). Like sage, it grows well in soil that is on the dry side, and it has a shrubby profile that, with age, gains a semiwoody base. The flowers, carried in loose whorls, are very pretty, usually a vibrant shade of deep purple, though lighter ones often appear. You can also find hyssop flowers in white and pink. They make a lovely contribution to any herb garden, and attract bees and butterflies.

Hyssop has been in cultivation a long, long time. Though it is mentioned by name in the Bible, experts agree that marjoram or a similar plant was probably meant instead, as hyssop doesn't grow wild in the Middle East. In years past, hyssop was often used as a strewing herb. Its pungency also made for good, strong teas administered to people suffering from a sore throat, bronchitis, or even asthma. These days, you occasionally find it in natural cold remedies. You may also see it as an ingredient in the aromatic liqueurs Benedictine and Chartreuse. And modern science has found that the plant has antiviral properties—in fact, AIDS researchers are taking a closer look at it.

Jerusalem sage

Phlomis fruticosa

HEIGHT/WIDTH: 2'–4' × 1'–3' (60–120cm × 30–90cm)

FLOWERS/BLOOM TIME: yellow/early summer

ZONES: 5–10

RECOMMENDED USES: craft

Jerusalem sage

A lovely, low-maintenance choice for the herb or flower garden, Jerusalem sage grows into a pleasantly scented, much-branched plant. The gray leaves are large (up to 4 inches [10cm] long), lance-shaped, wrinkled, and velvety to the touch. Unlike those of many of its relatives, Jerusalem sage's flowers are not in the blue and purple range, but rather a sunny lemon yellow. They're borne in whorls along the erect stems and are about an inch (2.5cm) across. They dry beautifully, which endears them to makers of wreaths, dried bouquets, and potpourris.

Grow this handsome plant in full sun or partial shade in well-drained soil that is on the dry side; a slope is an excellent setting. Don't neglect it completely, though—a little supplementary water inspires robust flowering. In mild climates, Jerusalem sage remains evergreen over the winter; to keep it from becoming scraggly, cut it back by one-third to one-half each autumn. In other climes, it dies back to the ground but returns with gusto the following spring.

Johnny jump-up

Viola tricolor

HEIGHT/WIDTH: 6″–12″ × 4″–8″ (15–30cm × 10–20cm)

FLOWERS/BLOOM TIME: purple and yellow or
white/summer

ZONES: all zones (annual)

RECOMMENDED USES: culinary, craft

Johnny jump-up

The common name for this sweet, tufted little plant comes from its ability to catapult seeds every which way when its ripe pod bursts open. This enthusiastic shower of seeds leads to new plants "jumping up" in unexpected places around the yard.

In rich, moist soil, you are sure to have plenty of plants, and may adopt a rather indulgent attitude toward them, as they are so small and charming. The flowers, generally no more than an inch (2.5cm) across, are usually of three colors: petals of purple, blue, and creamy white are accented with tiny "whisker" markings radiating from a yellow center. The leaves become heart-shaped as they mature.

The pansylike flowers are edible, and are pretty in salads or as a garnish for dips, soups, or omelets. Pinch one out and taste it alone and you will detect a bubble-gum flavor. Johnny jump-up flowers also candy well and make lovely decorations for special cakes. (Gingerly brush freshly harvested blossoms with a water/egg white mixture, then sprinkle with white sugar and allow to dry.)

Another common name for this violet is hearts-ease, which refers to its long-ago reputation as a heart stimulant. The preparation and techniques have not survived to this day, and it may have been purely folklore, as other related violets were never touted for this ability.

Lady's mantle

Alchemilla vulgaris

HEIGHT/WIDTH: 1'–2' × 1½' (30–60cm × 45cm)

FLOWERS/BLOOM TIME: chartreuse/spring

ZONES: 4–7

RECOMMENDED USES: medicinal, dye

Lady's mantle

Alchemilla translates from the Latin as "little magical one," an indication of this long-popular plant's reputation. The broad lime green leaves are soft to the touch. When rain or early-morning dew gathers on them, the water beads up like quicksilver and sparkles—a unique and enchanting sight.

But the magic may also refer to the plant's medicinal uses. Infusions made from the leaves have been used to treat a wide range of female problems, from reducing heavy menstrual flows to easing cramping to regulating fluctuating hormone levels just after childbirth or during menopause. The leaves also yield a green dye for wool. And the fresh root, pressed against a cut, has been used to halt bleeding.

Even if you never avail yourself of these interesting uses, you will cherish the plant for the soft yet elegant beauty it brings to your herb garden. The scalloped leaves (up to 4 inches [10cm] across) are wide as herb leaves go, adding nice contrast. The frothy flowers, in a sharp, clear shade of yellow-green, appear in profusion each spring on short stalks that hold them slightly away from the leaves. Try lady's mantle as an edging plant to soften the straight lines of the garden's layout or to skirt a central birdbath or sundial.

This plant is easy to grow and adapts well to sun and partial shade alike, provided it gets well-drained but moist soil. If your summers are hot and dry, coddle it with fertile soil, some shade, and extra water.

Lavender, English

Lavandula angustifolia

HEIGHT/WIDTH: 2′–3′ × 2′–3′ (60–90cm × 60–90cm)

FLOWERS/BLOOM TIME: purple/summer

ZONES: 5–9

RECOMMENDED USES: cosmetic, craft, medicinal,

repellent

'Dutch' lavender

Beloved the world over for its delightful, penetrating fragrance, lavender surely is an herb-garden classic. There are several species and many cultivars, including ones with rosy flowers and white flowers, ones with foliage that is more green than gray, and especially compact or dwarf ones. But the quintessential hardy lavender, the one that has the strongest scent and makes the finest dried flowers and oil, remains good old English lavender. It grows best in light, well-drained soil with a higher pH. (If your soil is acidic, try adding lime dust or chips to the planting area.)

Many gardeners like to grow lavender as an edging plant or as a low hedge, uses that suit it very well. Even when it matures and develops a somewhat woody base, it retains a tidy, even graceful appearance. Shearing or clipping is a pleasant chore and one from which the plant recovers quickly. If you want to use the harvest, prune either just as the flowers are opening or when they are completely full. Dry them in a hot, dark place such as a garage or attic.

You may already be thinking of lavender for homemade potpourris and sachets, but it has many other uses. The leaves really do repel insects and moths, which is why sprigs are tucked into linen closets and chests. The yellowish oil, which is collected by boiling the flowers, can be added to baths to soothe dry skin and sore muscles. A few drops in hot tea act as a sedative. Both the dried flowers and the oil continue to be popular ingredients in all sorts of soaps, creams, and perfumes.

Lemon balm

Melissa officinalis

HEIGHT/WIDTH: 2'–3' × 1'–2' (60–90cm × 30–60cm)

FLOWERS/BLOOM TIME: pale yellow/summer

ZONES: 5–9

RECOMMENDED USES: medicinal, culinary

Lemon balm

Not an especially interesting-looking plant, lemon balm nonetheless distinguishes itself with other praiseworthy qualities. It is perhaps the most lemony of all the plants in the mint family and isn't nearly as invasive as its relatives. It spreads sideways, with a trailing habit. The plant does self-sow, so keep after it if you don't want an ever-expanding crop. Grow it in rich, moist—but very well drained—soil. And if you're able to provide partial shade, the plant will be more lush. You'll notice that bees adore the flowers, small and inconspicuous as they are.

Lemon balm is at its strongest when picked just as the tiny flowers begin to open. Chopped into green or fruit salads, it adds a welcome tang. Some chefs also prize it for baked or broiled fish dishes. A tasty yet mild tea brewed from lemon balm calms cold and flu symptoms, fevers, and tension headaches. (It is said that a thirteenth-century English nobleman who lived to be 108 had a cup of lemon balm tea nearly every day of his life. This story has almost certainly helped popularize the tea.) In any event, always use lemon balm fresh—dried leaves lose their flavor.

Lemongrass

Cymbopogon citratus

HEIGHT/WIDTH: 4'–6' × 2' (120–180cm × 60cm)

FLOWERS/BLOOM TIME: greenish clusters/summer

ZONES: 8–10

RECOMMENDED USES: culinary, medicinal, insect
repellent

Lemongrass

Lemongrass is a true grass, though it grows taller and denser than many of the ornamental grasses we are used to inviting into our gardens. It is native to the hot, humid tropics of southern India, Sri Lanka, and Ceylon, where it is known as serah. It rarely flowers or sets seed, so it is raised from divisions, which come with a small bulbous root. Gardeners in the Deep South or West ought to be able to raise it; the rest of us can bring it into a warm greenhouse for the winter or try it as a houseplant (it will grow smaller when confined to a pot). In any event, keep it well watered.

The broad blades emit a strong lemon scent when cut or broken. In fact, lemongrass is related to citronella and also repels mosquitoes, flies, and fleas. But it is best known as an essential ingredient in Indonesian and Thai cuisine, where it enhances everything from coconut milk–based soups to stir-fries. Your homegrown lemongrass will certainly add splendor to such dishes.

Lemongrass also makes a pleasant, soothing tea. It has been used to treat all sorts of disorders, including indigestion, fever, colds, and headaches. The oil has been shown to lower high blood pressure as well as inhibit blood coagulation, so look for this herb to be of continued interest to the medical world.

Lemon verbena

Aloysia triphylla

HEIGHT/WIDTH: 6′–10′ × 3′–6′ (180–300cm × 90–180cm)

FLOWERS/BLOOM TIME: white spikes/summer

ZONES: 8–10

RECOMMENDED USES: culinary, cosmetic

Lemon verbena

Not a leafy herb at all but rather a robust shrub, lemon verbena holds an important place in the worlds of herbal cosmetics and cooking. The useful part is the lime green leaves, which sport a delicate lemon aroma when touched. Cooks like to add the fresh or dried leaves to all sorts of recipes, from fish and chicken to desserts. As you might guess, the leaves are also great for a sweet tea. It used to be a tradition to place a sprig next to finger bowls at fancy meals. Lemon verbena is also an ingredient in some citrusy colognes; you may wish to steep sprigs in a hot bath.

Native to South America, this tender shrub is not very hardy up north. However, gardeners in mild areas of North America have succeeded in growing it, with winter protection when warranted. It also takes well to life in a tub, so gardeners in other areas can grow it if they don't mind hauling it indoors each autumn. It will drop its leaves, but then rebound the following spring.

Lemon verbena needs full sun, does best in rich, moist soil, and should never be overwatered. With age, the plant becomes leggy, so underplant it with something shorter and unscented (so that there'll be no competition for your nose). Some gardeners have had fun capitalizing on this tendency towards legginess by pruning their plant to look like a big lollipop. The plant is vulnerable to spider mites and whiteflies, so keep it in good health as a preventative measure, and go to battle against the pests quickly should they appear.

Licorice

Glycyrrhiza glabra

HEIGHT/WIDTH: 3'–7' × 2'–4' (90–210cm × 60–120cm)

FLOWERS/BLOOM TIME: purple spikes/midsummer

ZONES: 8–10

RECOMMENDED USES: culinary, medicinal, cosmetic

Licorice

If you are a fan of licorice candy, you may be surprised to learn that you have not been enjoying the real thing. The little black candies and ropy twists are actually flavored with milder anise. Most true licorice—derived from the pungent root of a rangy member of the pea family—is imported into North America to enhance the flavor of tobacco products, including chew, cigarettes, and snuff.

In its native Mediterranean and Asia, sticks of licorice root continue to be popular as a sweet snack food and to slake thirst. Over the centuries, the plant has been employed in a wide range of remedies, but recent studies of some of these uses have raised red flags. In particular, the active ingredient glycyrrhizin has been implicated in causing high blood pressure, salt and water retention, cardiac arrest, kidney failure, and paralysis. In small doses in over-the-counter treatments, though, licorice is still considered safe and effective in cough syrups and lozenges and as a digestive aid that limits acid production. It's also an effective shampoo additive for those with oily hair.

Should you wish to try your hand at growing it, be sure to give it an out-of-the-way spot where it can spread, partly because it isn't especially attractive, but also because once planted it's hard to eradicate. It needs rich, well-drained, deep soil in full or partial shade. Generally raised from cuttings, it takes up to four years to develop a mature, usable root.

Lovage

Levisticum officinale

HEIGHT/WIDTH: 4′–6′ × 2′–3′ (120–180cm × 6090cm)

FLOWERS/BLOOM TIME: tiny yellow umbels/summer

ZONES: 4–9

RECOMMENDED USES: culinary, medicinal

Lovage

Although not directly related to celery, lovage looks and tastes a bit like it—but best of all, it's much easier to grow. Lovage is a tall and vigorous perennial, so plan on giving it the elbow room it needs toward the back of your garden. It is tricky to raise from seeds (they sprout slowly and irregularly), so buy young plants instead. Plant them in a site with full sun. The soil should be rich and well drained, especially if you are planning to harvest the tasty roots; it should also be on the sweet side. Mulch the area to conserve moisture and keep weeds at bay. By the second season, your lovage will be ready to supply you with a hearty harvest.

All parts of the lovage plant are edible. The flavor is hard to describe. It resembles celery but is stronger and, to some palates, "warmer." For this reason, it's a better choice for adding to stocks, soups, stews, and casseroles. It's a favorite for potato dishes, from basic mashed to cold potato salad. Experiment to see which parts you find tastiest—the tender young leaves, the mature stems, the stout root, or the savory seeds.

The one medicinal use that has stood the test of time is using the fresh or dried root to brew a diuretic tea (though pregnant women and people with kidney problems should not use it).

Lungwort

Pulmonaria officinalis

HEIGHT/WIDTH: 1′ × 1′–2′ (30cm × 30–60cm)

FLOWERS/BLOOM TIME: pink to blue/spring

ZONES: 3–9

RECOMMENDED USES: medicinal

'Bertram Anderson' lungwort

According to medieval doctrine, plants or plant parts that resembled body parts had a connection with those body parts. Thus the pretty, oval-shaped, cream-dappled leaves of this plant were associated with the lungs. Lungwort was used in folk medicine in Europe and Russia to treat minor bronchial congestion as well as bronchitis and even tuberculosis. These days, the evidence in its favor is weak. But the plant has been found to contain allantoin, a protein also found in comfrey that helps regenerate damaged tissue. Products containing allantoin are used to ease everything from athlete's foot to sores and burns. Lungwort's astringent properties are also used to treat diarrhea and hemorrhoids.

But for most herb gardeners, the real reason to grow this plant—and any of its charming relatives, especially Bethlehem sage (*P. saccharata*)—is its beauty. It grows well in partial shade and the leaf markings help it to stand out. The small, tubular flowers are also lovely, starting out rosy pink and opening to violet-blue. Because lungwort blooms in spring, it is a nice addition to a bulb garden, or it can be among the first signs of life each year in your herb garden.

Marjoram, sweet

Origanum majorana

HEIGHT/WIDTH: $1'–2' \times 1'–2'$ (30–60cm $\times$ 30–60cm)

FLOWERS/BLOOM TIME: white or pink/midsummer

ZONES: 6–9

RECOMMENDED USES: culinary

Marjoram

Marjoram is not oregano, but because they are related and resemble each other, people continue to confuse the two herbs. The main differences are in the flavor (marjoram is sweeter and more balsamlike) and the hardiness (marjoram is a more tender plant). It originally hails from the Mediterranean.

No matter where you live, though, you are bound to notice that it grows slowly and is not a large plant. For these reasons, you ought to start the tiny seeds indoors early or buy small plants when getting started. Marjoram likes full sun and decent, well-drained soil that is on the alkaline side. It can easily be overwhelmed by more vigorous plants,

including weeds, so coddle it until it hits its stride. If you live in a mild climate, bring it through the winter outdoors by mulching it, or just start over each year.

The best time to harvest the delicious leaves is just as the small flowers appear. If you cut the plant back to within an inch (2.5cm) or so of the ground, expect a second, lusher crop later in the season. Marjoram, unlike some herbs, keeps its full flavor even after it has been dried.

Cooks prize marjoram for all sorts of recipes. Try it in Italian dishes where you would usually use oregano. It is also a better choice for meat dishes (especially lamb) and a favorite in omelettes and homemade sausages.

Mexican lemon hyssop

Agastache mexicana

HEIGHT/WIDTH: 2′ × 1′–2′ (60cm × 30–60cm)

FLOWERS/BLOOM TIME: purple spikes/late summer

ZONES: 9–10

RECOMMENDED USES: culinary

'Giant Lemon' Mexican lemon hyssop

Not a hyssop at all but rather a member of the mint family and a close relative of anise hyssop, Mexican lemon hyssop has a bold mint-lemon scent and taste. A bushy plant that branches at the top, Mexican lemon hyssop sports fragrant, smooth, lance-shaped leaves. The appealing flowers, carried in spikes, are about 4 inches (10cm) long, tubular, and rosy pink to reddish purple.

As the name suggests, it is a native of Mexico, and thus it is not very hardy. However, it grows readily from seed and flowers its first summer, so gardeners in more northern zones can still enjoy it. They'll just need to treat it like an annual or dig it up each autumn to overwinter indoors. It does best in full sun and is not fussy about soil.

Use Mexican lemon hyssop leaves fresh or dried in hot or iced tea, summer drinks, sangria, and festive punches. The leaves also add an exotic, savory flavor to lamb dishes. You'll find that the flowers are just as tasty, and make a nice addition to salads and cold soups or as garnishes.

Mexican mint marigold

Tagetes lucida

HEIGHT/WIDTH: 2′–3′ × 1′–2′ (60–90cm × 30–60cm)

FLOWERS/BLOOM TIME: gold/autumn to winter

ZONES: 7–10

RECOMMENDED USES: culinary, craft, medicinal

Mexican mint marigold

Gardeners in areas with hot summers will cherish this perky little plant, not just for its beauty but also for its scented and tasty foliage, which is often likened to tarragon. And unlike French tarragon, Mexican mint marigold can take the heat. A rather small, clump-forming plant, this Mexican native blooms late in the season and continues until cool weather slows it down. It may bloom too sparsely or too late for gardeners in the North, but those with mild autumns and winters appreciate its cheerful and bountiful color. It's at its best when grown in full sun and moist but well-drained soil.

The flowers are not large—only about half an inch (12mm) across—but their warm golden orange color really stands out. They can be collected, dried, and brewed for a sweet-scented hot tea that eases cold symptoms and stomach woes. Known for retaining their color fairly well, the flowers are often included in dried wreaths, bouquets, and potpourris. If you let the flowers go to seed, you'll have many more plants next year—but you may appreciate this in case winter kills your original plants.

As for the lance-shaped leaves, they are dark green and bluntly toothed, and have a sweet, almost aniselike fragrance. Fresh leaves are wonderful in any recipe that calls for tarragon, including chicken, seafood, and veal dishes. They are sweet enough to be used in cool summer drinks and desserts (try them in fruit salad and sorbet).

Mexican oregano

Poliomintha longiflora

HEIGHT/WIDTH: 4'–6' × 3'–4' (120–180cm × 90–120cm)

FLOWERS/BLOOM TIME: pink-lavender, tubular/summer

ZONES: 8–10

RECOMMENDED USES: culinary

Mexican oregano

A handsome shrub that is sometimes used as a landscape hedge or foundation plant, Mexican oregano is also edible and makes a worthy substitute for regular oregano. It thrives in full sun and adapts to rich and dry soils alike. The glossy, oblong leaves are rather small—only about half an inch (12mm) long—and have a spicy, pungent scent much like oregano, though a bit sharper. They're delicious fresh or dried. Many cooks use them in tomato-based sauces and chili and they also make a wonderful contribution to stewed or roasted meats and marinated vegetables.

As an ornamental, the plant is quite pretty. It blooms prolifically once established, literally covering itself with small, tubular blossoms that vary from pink to lavender. In fact, sometimes the show is so heavy that the branches bend or sag under the weight. The flowers also attract a steady stream of bees, hummingbirds, and butterflies.

Mexican oregano prefers full sun and average soil. It can take a frost, but if grown north of Zone 9 it may not stay evergreen over the winter, and will appreciate a protective mulch. You can certainly cut it back, right to ground level, and watch for it to revive the following spring. If it is tender in your area, try digging up the plant and overwintering it indoors or taking stem cuttings in late summer.

Mint

Mentha spp.

HEIGHT/WIDTH: 1′–3′ × 1′–3′ (30–90cm × 30–90cm)

FLOWERS/BLOOM TIME: white, pink, or lavender spikes/midsummer

ZONES: 5–9

RECOMMENDED USES: culinary, medicinal

Spearmint

Refreshing mint is wonderful in all seasons—in summer, the fresh leaves are terrific in everything from mint juleps and iced tea to tabouli salad; in winter, the dried leaves make a warming tea (just for the pleasure of sipping or to treat sore throats and colds) and enhance lamb dishes and steamed vegetables. And creative cooks have come up with dozens of other ideas.

Mint's popularity is not just due to its flavor. It is also adaptable and extremely easy to grow. All it really needs is adequate water. Yes, its reputation for invasiveness is well earned. In fact, if mint has plenty of water—say, in a spot by a pond or stream—it will spread frighteningly fast. But its eager growth is a virtue if you plan to harvest often. Contain it by sinking a barrier around the outer limits of

where you want it to stay (try bricks or metal edging), or plant it in a pot and plunge that into the ground. The flowers, borne in clusters to form small spikes, vary in color from white to light purple; you can trim them off if you don't care for their looks.

There are literally hundreds of different mints, some of which are hard to distinguish from one another. The two most widely grown are, of course, peppermint (*M.* × *piperita*) and the shorter, somewhat sweeter spearmint (*M. spicata*). There are varieties of these, including variegated selections, as well as many closely related species. Shop around and try whatever appeals to you.

Mountain mint

Pycnanthemum muticum

HEIGHT/WIDTH: 2′–3′ × 1′-2′ (60–90cm × 30–60cm)

FLOWERS/BLOOM TIME: silvery pink/summer

ZONES: 5–9

RECOMMENDED USES: culinary

Mountain mint

This species—not a true mint—is native to eastern North America and enjoyed wide popularity until *Mentha* was introduced and overtook it. However, it is not nearly as aggressive and will grow well in drier soil. Also, the habit is more upright than spreading; over the years, it will form a handsome, multistemmed clump. So you can rest easy if you invite mountain mint into the herb garden proper.

The leaves radiate a fresh, minty scent that makes them suitable substitutes for true mint. Carried close to the plant on short stems, they're 2½ inches (6cm) long and medium green. The long-lasting pompon flowers are especially pretty—light pink to white, in a ruff of silvery bracts.

In the West, another plant goes by this name and shares the same qualities of easy growth and handsome appearance. Western mountain mint (*Agastache urticifolia*) is not a true mint, either. Related to anise and lemon hyssop, it grows 3 feet (90cm) tall and sports large, pink, fragrant blooms and minty foliage. Brewed hot, it makes a splendid, aromatic after-dinner tea.

Mugwort

Artemisia vulgaris

HEIGHT/WIDTH: 5'–6' × 1'–2' (150–180cm × 30–60cm)

FLOWERS/BLOOM TIME: tiny, reddish brown/ midsummer

ZONES: 4–9

RECOMMENDED USES: culinary, medicinal, craft

Mugwort

Slender, unprepossessing mugwort may not look special, but a great deal of folklore swirls around it. In the Middle Ages, people believed that wearing a wreath of it would protect them from evil spirits. In China, swags were hung over doorways for the same reason. The common name's origins are muddled; "wort" means plant, but the "mug" part is a mystery. It has been attributed to everything from midge or maggot (the plant does have insect-repelling abilities) to the cup that holds beer (it has been used in brewing in England and Ireland). And to this day, some acupuncturists use little wads of the leaf to burn a small spot on their patients' skin before inserting the needles.

From a modern gardener's point of view, however, mugwort is simply a graceful, easy to grow, sage-scented herb. It likes full sun and grows in most soils (though in damp soil it will spread rapidly). The leaves, up to 4 inches (10cm) long, are gray-green on top, cottony white below. They are perhaps too bitter for some palates, although European cooks have used small amounts in stuffings and sausages. Teas are not recommended for consumption because the plant contains the same toxins found in its notorious cousin wormwood or absinthe (*A. absinthum*).

A poultice made from the leaves, however, is effective in reducing inflammation, including a flare-up of poison oak or ivy. The leaves may also be dried and used to stuff a soothing sleep pillow.

Mullein

Verbascum thapsus

HEIGHT/WIDTH: 6′–8′ × 2′–3′ (180–240cm × 60–90cm)

FLOWERS/BLOOM TIME: yellow spikes/late summer

ZONES: 3–8

RECOMMENDED USES: medicinal

Mullein

Probably just about the tallest herb in the garden, stately mullein is easy to grow and softens its imposing appearance with broad, woolly leaves. Many people think it is a native roadside weed, but it is actually an ancient plant native to Europe and Asia that has escaped in North America. In a garden, you may want only one or two plants, but with a little attention to siting (a focal point in the middle of a sunny area, or a backdrop for a wall or hedge) and minimal care, mullein will provide great drama.

The plant is a biennial, which means that you get only foliage the first year, which is then joined the next year by that great, yellow flower-studded stalk. Let it shed its seeds if you want mullein beyond that point; otherwise, it will have exhausted itself and won't return the third year.

The leaves are a great attraction with mullein. They are large, sage-green, and fuzzy to the touch. As they ascend, they get smaller—apparently this design enables the plant to spill rain down to its lower levels and eventually to its roots.

Mullein has been used to treat respiratory problems, as a diuretic, and to ease gastronomic distress. However, the topical uses are more commonly employed these days. An extract of the flowers, mixed with oil, reduces the inflammation and pain of insect bites, earaches, and bruises.

Musk mallow

Malva moschata

HEIGHT/WIDTH: 2'–4' × 2'–3' (60–120cm × 60–90cm)

FLOWERS/BLOOM TIME: pale pink or white/summer

ZONES: 3–10

RECOMMENDED USES: medicinal

Musk mallow

Like its cousin hollyhock, musk mallow has simple, finely veined, five-petaled flowers (in softest pink to almost transparent white). But unlike hollyhock, this plant is compact and bushy. It gets the "musk" part of its name from the pleasant fragrance emitted when you rub or crush the light green leaves. An old-world plant, it was brought over by the earliest colonists, who cherished it for its prettiness, its long blooming period, and a number of folk remedies, most of which have been forgotten.

All of the plant parts contain a sap that produces a soothing mucilage, so like many other herbs, it makes a comforting tea. A poultice made from the leaves and stems was used to treat inflammations and insect bites.

Musk mallow asks little of the gardener, save well-drained soil. It grows well in full sun or partial shade and gets by with minimal maintenance. However, if you cut it back after it flowers, it will quickly rebloom. It also will self-sow.

Mustard

Brassica spp.

HEIGHT/WIDTH: 3′–6′ × 2′–4′ (90–180cm × 60–120cm)

FLOWERS/BLOOM TIME: yellow/summer

ZONES: all zones (annual)

RECOMMENDED USES: culinary, medicinal

'Giant Red' brown mustard

When you grow your own mustard seed, you are in for a special treat. Your harvest will have a fresh tang quite unlike the musty seeds you find in jars on store shelves. And, happily, mustard is very easy and fast-growing. It likes full sun and fertile soil, but will still produce a good crop in less-than-ideal conditions. Sow the previous autumn for an early summer harvest; sow in early spring for a mid-summer harvest. Cut down the stalks as soon as you notice the pods turning from green to brown, and lay them to dry so that you can collect their bounty. Be forewarned: plants left in the garden will self-sow.

There are three basic kinds of mustard in cultivation. The most familiar is white, or tan, mustard (*B. hirta*). It has light cream-colored, mild seeds that are used straight, for mustard powder, and for making yellow mustard (which actually gets its color from the addition of turmeric). The flavor of brown mustard (*B. juncea*) is stronger and is released when the seeds are ground and mixed with a liquid, such as oil or wine. Black mustard (*B. nigra*) seeds are tiny, making them difficult to harvest. They have the most pungent flavor of the three.

You may have heard of "mustard plasters," the time-honored remedy for treating congestion. Powdered seed is mixed with water, oil, or even egg whites and then applied as a poultice to the chest. The paste literally heats up due to the active ingredients in the seeds. It should be applied through a cloth and should not be left on too long because it can eventually cause blistering.

Nasturtium

Tropaeolum majus

HEIGHT/WIDTH: 1′ × 2′ (30cm × 60cm)

FLOWERS/BLOOM TIME: orange, red, or yellow/summer

ZONES: all zones (annual)

RECOMMENDED USES: culinary

'Empress of India' nasturtium

The bright, cheerful flowers of nasturtiums are always welcome. They bloom continually all summer and they do especially well in dry, poor soil—a real boon for some gardeners! Not surprisingly, a plant this agreeable and charming is available in many forms. Look for climbing nasturtiums (which can either ascend a support or trail down from a deck or window box), ones with dappled (variegated) foliage, dwarf varieties, and pastel colors. Somewhere along the way, certain nasturtiums lost the spur in their flowers, which takes away some of the old-fashioned appeal.

Creative cooks prize nasturtiums. The large, roundish leaves, often used in salads, have a crunchy texture and boast ten times the vitamin C of lettuce! Their peppery taste reminds some people of watercress. The flowers (with the bitter pistils removed) have a similar flavor. You can also use the flowers as a pretty garnish, float some in a big bowl of party punch, or stuff them with cream cheese or tuna salad. Add the stems to simmering soups. The buds, pickled in vinegar, have been used as a piquant substitute for capers. Dried seeds can be ground and used as a pepper substitute.

Oregano

Origanum vulgare

HEIGHT/WIDTH: 1′–3′ × 1′–3′ (30–90cm × 30–90cm)

FLOWERS/BLOOM TIME: pink/midsummer

ZONES: 5–9

RECOMMENDED USES: culinary

'Aureum' and common oregano

Originally from the dry, sun-washed hillsides of Greece and Turkey, true oregano, when grown well, produces a richly fragrant, almost peppery crop unlike any other herb. The secret to success is to select your initial plants with care (raising from seed is risky because the plant is naturally variable). There are other species and many cultivars out there, plus a long-standing confusion with the similar-looking but milder-tasting marjoram. Some enthusiasts swear by *O. vulgare* ssp. *hirtum*, also known as *O. heracleoticum*; the cultivar 'Viride' has received a lot of praise as well. Whether you find these or not, let your nose be the judge—rub the leaves between your fingers and sniff as you hunt for the oregano of your dreams. Once you get it home, plant your oregano in conditions similar to its native habitat: warm, friable soil that is on the dry side. Hot weather increases the oil content, leading to a superb harvest.

To harvest, snip young leaves. The plant will generate more and, indeed, grow bushier. Although it dries and freezes well, use fresh oregano in your favorite recipes whenever possible.

Orris root

Iris × germanica var. florentina

HEIGHT/WIDTH: 1½'–2½' × 1'–2' (45–75cm × 30–60cm)

FLOWERS/BLOOM TIME: white/early summer

ZONES: 3–10

RECOMMENDED USES: cosmetic, craft

Orris root

It looks like a regular bearded iris, with its creamy white petals, purple-tinted falls, and golden beard, but this beauty is no ordinary iris. The difference is in the root, which was long ago discovered to harbor a unique, heady scent that has been likened to sweet violets. Not evident immediately upon harvesting, the fragrance becomes more potent the longer the root has been dried—and it may take up to two years to reach its finest potential.

At any rate, the dried root is pulverized to a powder, which is used in a variety of ways. It is mixed into perfumes and powders, and has been added to a shampoo that is supposed to be especially effective on oily hair. It is an ingredient in the famous Italian fragrance mixture frangipani.

Orris root powder also lends a wonderful, romantic quality to sachets and sleep pillows. In potpourris, it has the added quality of acting as a fixative.

Grow orris root as you would any other iris, in well-drained soil that is rich in organic matter and toward the alkaline side. Plant in late summer or autumn, placing the rhizome only halfway into the soil (otherwise it is likely to rot). When it flowers, cut the blooms for bouquets or promptly deadhead so that the plant puts maximum energy into root development. Harvest on a dry autumn day: dig up the roots, trim away the stems, scrub off all dirt, and lay them out to dry in a cool, dark, but ventilated location.

Parsley

Petroselinum crispum

HEIGHT/WIDTH: 1'–3' × 1'–3' (30–90cm × 30–90cm)

FLOWERS/BLOOM TIME: tiny greenish yellow
umbels/summer

ZONES: 4–9

RECOMMENDED USES: culinary, medicinal

Parsley

When you look out over your garden on a dreary winter day, you may be surprised to see one bright green spot—the parsley plant, lingering on. This herb is especially hardy and also a cinch to grow, thriving in full sun and average soil. But unless you have a lot of patience, you'd better raise it from small plants; the seeds are notoriously slow starters. Also, parsley is technically a biennial, which means that the survivor out there will still be there next spring and summer, though its second year is never as good as its first. In fact, it usually goes to seed and dies back. So easygoing is this herb, it has become popular with windowsill gardeners. Give it sun, as big a pot as practical, and regular water.

There are two popular kinds of parsley. The species is curly leaf; flat leaf is *P. crispum* var. *neapolitanum*. Experienced cooks will tell you that the latter has a stronger, richer flavor. (As a result, it dries better, although fresh parsley is generally preferable to dried.) Too often dismissed as a mere garnish, parsley is actually vitamin-packed and deserves to be eaten for that reason alone. It is rich in vitamins A and C, certain B vitamins, iron, and calcium. Use it to enrich many recipes, including stocks, soups, grilled meats, stuffings, casseroles, and vegetable dishes.

Parsley's most famous folk use is as a natural breath freshener, diminishing even the power of garlic. At one time, parsley brewed in a mild tea was considered to be an appetite stimulant. That may be true, but too much can damage the kidneys, so this use has fallen out of favor.

Patchouli

Pogostemon spp.

HEIGHT/WIDTH: 2'–4' × 2'–3' (60–120cm × 60–90cm)

FLOWERS/BLOOM TIME: White to pale purple/summer

ZONES: 9–10

RECOMMENDED USES: cosmetics, medicinal, insect
repellent

Patchouli

This attractive tropical plant, related to mint and native to India and the Philippines, is easily grown as a houseplant. It thrives in hot weather, so put it outside during the summer. In mild climates, it can be grown right in the ground in well-drained soil and will survive the winter with a light mulch. In any case, water patchouli regularly, and protect it from midday sun if the leaves show signs of sunburn. Two very similar species are available: *P. cablin*, which is up to 4 feet (1.2m) tall, and the more compact *P. heyneanus*, which is a little trickier to grow and must not be allowed to dry out.

Patchouli is grown for its glossy, slightly scalloped leaves. When rubbed, they release a spicy, incenselike scent. They retain their fragrance well when dried. Patchouli is a popular component of incense sticks, cones, and candles as well as potpourri blends. It has been used by Indian rug merchants to protect their products from moth damage. An oil derived from the leaves makes an earthy, penetrating perfume. The oil has also been used medicinally as an antiseptic. In larger doses, it is a sedative.

Pennyroyal, English

Mentha pulegium

HEIGHT/WIDTH: 4"–16" × 8"–18" (10–40cm × 20–45cm)

FLOWERS/BLOOM TIME: blue/summer

ZONES: 6–10

RECOMMENDED USES: insect repellent

Pennyroyal

If you're looking for a scented, mat-forming groundcover, perhaps in a sunny rock garden or as an edging for your herb beds, pennyroyal just may be your plant. A low-growing, many-branched mint, it creeps with lax runners that send down roots wherever they touch the soil. The foliage is dark green and sports an especially strong minty fragrance.

Unlike other mints, however, this one should never be ingested. In days gone by, it was used to induce vomiting, to treat fevers, and even to induce menstruation and abortion, but the dangers have proven to outweigh the benefits. It contains chemicals that are highly toxic, even in small doses—as little as an ounce (29.5ml) of the oil can bring on convulsions and even a coma!

Pennyroyal's claim to fame is that it repels insects—mosquitoes, fleas, ticks, chiggers, gnats, and biting flies, among others. Indeed, many bug sprays, lotions, and pet flea collars list it as a main ingredient. Leaves clipped from your homegrown plants can be rubbed on your skin before you go on a hike or picnic.

Pineapple sage

Salvia elegans

HEIGHT/WIDTH: 2′–4′ × 2′–3′ (60–120cm × 60–90cm)

FLOWERS/BLOOM TIME: red/late summer

ZONES: 7–10

RECOMMENDED USES: culinary

'Americana' pineapple sage

There are many, many sages, of course, but this one is unique for its sweet, inviting, ripe-pineapple scent. It's a bushy plant, and tends to require more water than some of its relatives. Although it's not very hardy, gardeners north of its range can still enjoy it as an annual or in a pot.

Pineapple sage also looks different from other sages, with softly hairy lime green leaves that are lightly toothed and rimmed in red, and often reddish stems. In late summer and autumn, it envelops itself in gorgeous, ruby red flowers. A wonderful cultivar now available, 'Frieda Dixon', has dusty, coral-red blooms. The flowers attract bees, butterflies, and hummingbirds.

The delicious scent and flavor make this plant suitable for all sorts of uses in the kitchen. Use both leaves and flowers in teas, green salads, and fruit salads, or add them to iced summer drinks (imagine pineapple sage sprigs as garnish for homemade piña coladas!). The dried leaves, which retain the distinctive scent well, make a novel addition to pork recipes and rice dishes.

Plantain

Plantago major

HEIGHT/WIDTH: 6″–12″ × 6″–12″ (15–30cm × 15–30cm)

FLOWERS/BLOOM TIME: tiny greenish spikes/summer

ZONES: 3–10

RECOMMENDED USES: medicinal

'Atropurpurea' plantain

In all truth, you are unlikely to plant plantain, but you should stop thinking of it as a nuisance weed when you encounter it in your lawn. An old-world import that has dispersed throughout North America, this super-hardy herb actually has a number of handy and verified medicinal uses.

Plantain, like dandelion, forms a ground-hugging rosette early in the season. The flower spikes appear later and aren't much to write home about—they look a bit like tiny cattails. They produce seeds quickly and spread them liberally, so here is your control measure if you don't want too much plantain: chop or mow off the spikes as soon as they appear.

The tough, fibrous, wide, oval-shaped leaves are the useful part of the plant and are easily distinguished from similar plants by their parallel veins. Their antiseptic properties have been valued for centuries. Crushed, they emit a pleasant, grassy scent and provide quick and soothing relief for insect bites and bee stings. Salves and poultices (sterilize the leaves first by dipping them briefly in boiling water) have been used to treat sores, wounds, and all sorts of dermatis, from heat rash to poison oak and ivy. In India, southeast Asia, and Russia, plantain has a long history of other uses, especially in the treatment of coughs, colds, bronchitis, and even asthma.

Rosemary

Rosmarinus officinalis

HEIGHT/WIDTH: 5'–6' × 3'–6' (150–180cm × 90–180cm); in a container, 1'–2' × 1'–2' (30–60cm × 30–60cm)

FLOWERS/BLOOM TIME: blue or pink/summer

ZONES: 8–10

RECOMMENDED USES: culinary, medicinal, cosmetic

Rosemary

On a long, hot summer afternoon, one herb plant still looks crisp and graceful and radiates a drowsy, piney scent as you brush by—that's rosemary. Because it hails from the dry hillsides and valleys of the Mediterranean, it is a sun lover, drought tolerant and adaptable to nearly any soil (though in an acidic soil, a little counteracting lime powder or wood ash is recommended). In mild climates, depending on the cultivar, it will grow slowly and spread over the years as a groundcover or semiwoody shrub. Try it as a foundation planting, trailing over a wall, or as a low hedge. In cooler climates, protect it from winter's cold with a mulch, or dig it up and overwinter it indoors. In a container, rosemary appreciates a light, sandy soil so that it can avoid root rot.

Harvest rosemary any time during the growing season (but if possible, pick before the plant flowers). The newest, youngest stems have the most fragrant and flavorful leaves. You'll find that rosemary dries and freezes well. Fresh or dried, it is a splendid addition to roasted meats and poultry, and dishes that feature tomatoes, squash, beans, or peas.

Potions derived from the leaves have been used for treating all sorts of ills, including headaches, infections, poor circulation, and poor digestion. Topically, an ointment is said to soothe the pain of rheumatism. You can toss some sprigs in a hot bath to soothe aching muscles. Shampoo with rosemary in it brings a fresh luster to dark hair.

Rue

Ruta graveolens

HEIGHT/WIDTH: 1'–3' × 1'–2' (30–90cm × 30–60cm)

FLOWERS/BLOOM TIME: tiny yellow clusters/summer

ZONES: 4–9

RECOMMENDED USES: medicinal ornamental

Rue

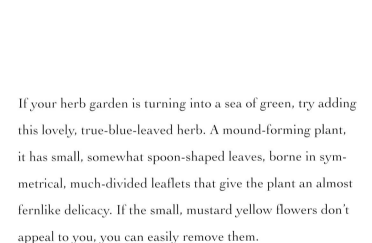

If your herb garden is turning into a sea of green, try adding this lovely, true-blue-leaved herb. A mound-forming plant, it has small, somewhat spoon-shaped leaves, borne in symmetrical, much-divided leaflets that give the plant an almost fernlike delicacy. If the small, mustard yellow flowers don't appeal to you, you can easily remove them.

Rue is simple to grow. It likes sandy or loamy soil best and is drought tolerant. Pests and diseases never bother it. The only thing to watch out for is possible dermatitis when handling the plants—some people develop a rash. Each spring, remember to chop it down to ground level so that the new growth will be more compact.

No doubt the unusual-looking and pungent leaves have added to the many beliefs and uses surrounding rue. It was used to ward off witches, evil spirits, and sinfulness, not to mention the Black Plague and epileptic seizures. Less colorful uses included treating digestion problems and promoting menstruation; recent studies have shown, however, that large doses of rue can be very dangerous, inducing vomiting, convulsions, and abortion. You are best off appreciating rue for its ornamental beauty, regaling garden visitors with these stories, and using it only as a striking addition to flower arrangements.

Safflower

Carthamus tinctorius

HEIGHT/WIDTH: $2'$–$3' \times 1'$–$2'$ (60–90cm $\times$ 30–60cm)

FLOWERS/BLOOM TIME: orange-yellow puffs/mid-summer to autumn

ZONES: all zones (annual)

RECOMMENDED USES: craft, dye, culinary

Safflower

This plant looks a bit like a thistle, with bristly leaves, spiny stems, and compact, round flowers. But what flowers! Their thin, tubular petals are electric orange-yellow. Not surprisingly, enterprising gardeners have found good uses for such bright color. They're terrific in potpourris, dried-flower arrangements, and wreaths. They also yield dyes in shades from scarlet to rose to yellow.

But perhaps the most intriguing use of the flowers is as a saffron substitute. As you may know, saffron is a small bulb plant whose harvest is quite small and therefore expensive. Dried and used as is or infused to make a concentrate, safflower can give cream sauces, soups, curries, rice dishes, and salad dressings that desirable reddish hue. The flavor, alas, is much weaker than saffron, so add extra if you're aiming for more than just the coloring effect. This is also the same plant that yields a quality low-cholesterol oil, though extracting it from the ripe seeds may be too ambitious a project for a home gardener.

To grow safflower, direct-sow the seeds in the garden in late spring in a spot that receives full sun. Average, well-drained soil is fine. You might want to place your crop out of the way a bit because of the prickles.

Sage

Salvia officinalis

HEIGHT/WIDTH: 1′–3′ × 1′–3′ (30–90cm × 30–90cm)

FLOWERS/BLOOM TIME: purple, pink, or white/summer

ZONES: 4–8

RECOMMENDED USES: culinary, medicinal

'Aurea' sage

Usually gray-green and always aromatic, sage is deservedly popular. And growing your own is especially satisfying because the plants are so easy to raise and the harvest is always pretty and delicious. They thrive in full sun and well-drained soil, are drought tolerant, and require little care once established. They should, however, be pruned back hard each spring to keep the plant's habit neat and manageable. Expect to replace them every few years, because with age they do tend to become woody and ragged-looking. Also, thanks to their handsome flower spikes (colors vary), you'll welcome plenty of butterflies and hummingbirds to your garden.

You can certainly remain with the plain old species, *S. officinalis*, but it has a number of appealing cultivars that will add to the beauty of your herb garden. There are also many worthy related species.

Sages of this species, however, are not strictly decorative and will do double duty in the kitchen. Fresh leaves can be used in stuffings, vegetable dishes, casseroles, egg dishes, soups, and sausages. Both flowers and leaves can be used as garnishes, fresh or candied. The leaves dry well, though the flavor loses some of its subtlety. Store dried sage leaves in a dry, airtight container out of sunlight and away from heat.

Medicinal uses abound, from drinking the soothing tea at bedtime or to ease a sore throat to making a salve for treating sores, cuts, and bruises. Apparently, sage is also useful as an antiperspirant and has been proven to lower blood sugar in diabetics.

Savory, Summer

Satureja hortensis

HEIGHT/WIDTH: 12″–18″ × 12″–18″ (30–45cm × 30–45cm)

FLOWERS/BLOOM TIME: white to pale pink/summer

ZONES: all zones (annual)

RECOMMENDED USES: culinary

Savory

What would homemade potato salad or freshly steamed green beans be without a fresh sprinkling of minced summer savory leaves? This herb has a wonderful, peppery tang that adds a finishing touch to so many dishes. When you harvest often, the plant is prevented from flowering (which slows growth) and continues to pump out a great supply of lanky stems lined with tiny, 1-inch (2.5cm) -long leaves all summer long.

Summer savory is easy to raise from seed, germinating quickly and growing eagerly. In the garden, all it requires is full sun, occasional water, and well-drained soil. In a container garden or window box, don't neglect watering, and clip often so that the plant's floppy stems remain within bounds.

If you enjoy summer savory, you might also try its close relative, winter savory (*S. montana*). This is a short-lived perennial plant, hardy to Zone 6. It grows shorter and yields similar but stronger-flavored leaves.

To dry summer or winter savory leaves, lay them on a screen or paper in a warm, shaded location. When they're ready, zip them off the stems and store in an airtight jar. Bring them out to dress up soups and stews containing beans and lentils or to mix into an herb butter. They're also great with roasts and in all sorts of vegetable dishes.

Self-heal

Prunella vulgaris

HEIGHT/WIDTH: 12″–18″ × 8″–12″ (30–45cm × 20–30cm)

FLOWERS/BLOOM TIME: purple/summer

ZONES: 4–9

RECOMMENDED USES: medicinal, dye

Self-heal

A plant with a name like this must have a great reputation as a healing herb, and so it does—or did in times gone by. Also known as all-heal, this mint relative has been used for a wide range of treatments. Topically, a salve or poultice was used on cuts, burns, rashes, and bleeding hemorrhoids. Taken internally, it was used to reduce high fevers and as a diuretic. A gentle tea brewed from the leaves was also touted as a soothing gargle for gum inflammations or a sore throat, to ease laryngitis, and as a mouthwash. None of these uses for self-heal has been studied carefully in modern times, though they remain popular folk remedies. Another use for self-heal is as a dye plant. Depending on the strength of the infusion, the leaves produce a soft yellow to golden color in various fabrics.

Self-heal is an agreeable garden plant. A creeping mat-former, it is not terribly invasive. It does best in full sun, becoming raggedy and leggy in partial or full shade, and it grows more vigorously in damp soil. It makes a good groundcover. The flowers, like most members of the mint family, are purplish and not showy.

Sesame

Sesamum indicum

HEIGHT/WIDTH: 2′–3′ × 1′–2′ (60–90cm × 30–60cm)

FLOWERS/BLOOM TIME: white to purple/summer

ZONES: 8–10 (annual in other zones)

RECOMMENDED USES: culinary

Sesame

Grow your own sesame seeds? Why not? This handsome, easygoing plant is a tropical native and looks like it, with ample, lance-shaped 5-inch (12.5cm) leaves and showy, drooping 1-inch (2.5cm) -long flowers in shades of purple to pink to white. It can be grown outdoors in warm climates, such as the South and Gulf Coast, and as an annual in more northern zones. Sesame's main requirement is sufficient water, so don't allow it to dry out.

The flowers, if given a long enough season, fade away to 1-inch (2.5cm) -long brown capsules that contain those tasty, nutty, flat seeds in abundance—about a tablespoon per pod. The seeds are an excellent source of protein and carbohydrates as well as phosphorus, niacin, and sulfur. They can be ground up into a paste called tahini, a popular condiment or cooking ingredient in Middle Eastern cuisine. Of course, fresh or lightly toasted, the seeds are also a great addition to breads, rolls, and bagels, and can be tossed over fresh salads or used to flavor soups and casseroles.

Sesame seeds also provide an edible oil, called sesame or "gingelly" oil, that is valued for its rich flavor.

Shiso

Perilla frutescens

HEIGHT/WIDTH: 1′–3′ × 1′–3′ (30–90cm × 30–90cm)

FLOWERS/BLOOM TIME: pinkish spikes/summer

ZONES: all zones (annual)

RECOMMENDED USES: culinary

'Crispa' shiso

Although this plant resembles the ordinary houseplant or edging plant coleus, shiso is not to be underestimated. Long a staple of Asian cookery, it is versatile, has wonderful flavor, and is quite attractive in its own right. The glossy leaves, which have a distinctively spicy taste and crunchy texture, may be added to fresh salads, marinated salads, and tempura. The leaves are not used dried. The flower spikes flavor cold and hot soups. The seeds are salted and added to vinegar, dressings, pickles, and tempura. They're also sometimes served as a meal-ending savory.

Shiso comes in two forms. The green form, called 'Crispa', is a bright spring green with ruffled edges. The red, or purple, form, called 'Atropurpurea', has a nearly metallic sheen. Both are beautiful in the garden and are sure to excite comments from visitors. Both forms grow best in rich, well-drained soil, and although they are annuals, they'll self-sow. During the growing season, harvest the leaves often and remove the flowerstalks as they appear; this pruning will keep the plants fuller and bushier.

Sorrel, French

Rumex acetosa

HEIGHT/WIDTH: 12″–36″ × 8″–24″ (30–90cm × 20–60cm)

FLOWERS/BLOOM TIME: reddish-green spikes/summer

ZONES: 5–9

RECOMMENDED USES: culinary

Sorrel

One of the quintessential treats of summer is savory, lemony cream-of-sorrel soup, served cold outdoors on the back porch. Its main ingredient is an undistinguished, weedy-looking perennial plant with broad, arrow-shaped, bright green leaves clustered at the base and ascending a crisp, juicy, reddish stalk. The leaves get their sharp flavor principally from the presence of oxalic acid and vitamin C.

The best harvest comes when summer is well under way—immature leaves don't have the tangy flavor. Harvest in the morning when the plants are at their most succulent, and puree for soup or other dishes. The leaves are also wonderful diced into salads and cheese omelettes and added to fish recipes. Some people like to steam them like spinach.

Growing sorrel is not difficult. It does best in fertile, moist soil and appreciates a sheltered spot so that the wind doesn't batter the leaves. Sorrel is appealing to slugs, so if these pests are a problem in your yard, take steps to protect your crop (set out bait, copper strips, or wood ash).

Sweet Annie

Artemisia annua

HEIGHT/WIDTH: 5'–10' × 3'–5' (150–300cm × 90–150cm)

FLOWERS/BLOOM TIME: tiny pale yellow balls/summer

ZONES: all zones (annual)

RECOMMENDED USES: craft

Sweet Annie

A lovely, feathery, many-branched plant, sweet Annie smells just like ripe, sweet apples. Individual leaves, a soft shade of gray-green, are about 4 inches (10cm) long at most, but are much-divided and carried in such density on the plant that the effect is always lush. Later in the summer, they are joined by loose, nodding panicles of tiny flowers.

Sweet Annie grows quickly and does best in full sun and average soil. Because of its height and texture, it makes a wonderful backdrop or screen for other herbs or flowers. It is too graceful and fragrant to be considered a weed!

Cut the stems toward the end of the summer, before the plant goes to seed, and hang them upside down to dry in a cool, dark place. The leaves and tiny flowers will turn golden brown but retain that wonderful scent. Crafters like to fashion the long, flexible dried stems into a base for a delicate scented wreath or include short pieces in mixed wreaths. Of course, sweet Annie also makes a wonderful addition to dried-flower arrangements.

Sweet cicely

Myrrhis odorata

HEIGHT/WIDTH: 2′–3′ × 1′–2′ (60–90cm × 30–60cm)

FLOWERS/BLOOM TIME: white umbels/spring

ZONES: 3–8

RECOMMENDED USES: culinary

Sweet cicely

Unlike many herbs, sweet cicely grows well in shade and partial shade, and prefers moist soil. Certainly the lacy, fernlike foliage fits in well in such settings. Include the freshly harvested leaves in summertime meals, such as green salads or chicken, potato, or tuna salads. You'll find that it has a sweet, crisp, celery-anise flavor. Sweet cicely also makes a novel garnish.

The broad white flowers look like those of many other herbs. But they bloom in less than full sun and appear in the spring rather than the summer, attracting the early attention of foraging bees. The thin, ridged, ¾-inch (2cm) seeds are edible and may be eaten unripe or ripe. Unripe seeds are green and have a sweet, nutty flavor. They can be enjoyed on the spot or tossed into fruit salad or other desserts. Ripe ones are dark brown and glossy; used whole, they add great character to apple pie or pear tarts. They can also be crushed or powdered and stored in an airtight jar to be used later to sweeten baked goods such as sweet holiday breads and muffins.

The plant is best raised from store-bought seedlings or divisions donated by another gardener, as the seeds germinate slowly and erratically. It forms a thick, gnarled taproot, so plant it where you want it to stay.

Sweet woodruff

Galium odoratum

HEIGHT/WIDTH: 6″–12″ × 12″ (15–30cm × 30cm)

FLOWERS/BLOOM TIME: white stars/spring

ZONES: 3–9

RECOMMENDED USES: culinary, craft

Sweet woodruff

This enchanting plant makes a wonderful groundcover for full- to partial-shade areas in damp or dry soil. The long, thin, apple-green leaves occur in whorls and spread slowly but surely over the years. They are joined each spring by tiny, dainty flowers (only ¼ inch [6mm] across and white-to cream-colored). Both the leaves and flowers exude a sweet, grassy scent; when dried, the fragrance becomes noticeably more vanillalike.

Not surprisingly, there are many uses for this charmer. In Germany, it flavors May wine (*Mai Bowle*), a beverage that has been used for centuries in May Day celebrations.

To taste something similar to this treat, try immersing a few sprigs in a bottle of sweet white wine a day before you plan to serve it. At one time, sweet woodruff was also used to makes a scented hot tea intended to soothe upset stomachs. Recent studies have shown, alas, that this herb's active ingredient coumarin is dangerous in large quantities and is safe to consume only in the wine, not straight up. Sweet woodruff is also a natural addition to potpourris, and some craftspeople like to add clumps to the stuffing in pillows and mattresses.

Tansy

Tanacetum vulgare

HEIGHT/WIDTH: 3'–4' × 2'–3' (90–120cm × 60–90cm)

FLOWERS/BLOOM TIME: small yellow buttons/mid- to
late summer

ZONES: 4–9

RECOMMENDED USES: insect repellent, craft

Tansy

Here is a plant with a long and fascinating history. Often associated with royalty in the past, nowadays it's relegated to the status of an ornamental herb. The oldest story about it goes back to the Greek legends: lore has it that a drink made from tansy conferred immortality on a handsome young man named Ganymede so that he could serve as Zeus' cup bearer. Tansy was often used as a strewing herb; King James II had it spread along the road to his coronation ceremony.

No doubt about it—tansy has a strong personality. The pungent peppery pine scent is released when you brush past the plant or if you crush the leaves between your fingers. It has been employed, often with success, as an insect repellent—in particular, it is said to keep away ants and flies. Organic gardeners find it useful, too, especially in warding off the Colorado potato beetle.

The plant is an aggressive grower in full sun and average soil. It spreads quickly by means of underground rhizomes, so site it where you won't have to be constantly trying to rein it in. The flowers are a bright mustard yellow that stands out well in the garden. They dry fairly well and for this reason are used in dried wreathes, swags, and arrangements.

As for tansy's medicinal and culinary uses, these have fallen out of favor since the essential oil thujone was identified as a component of all the plant parts. Thujone damages the central nervous system and can cause seizures; it is potentially fatal to pregnant women.

Tarragon

Artemisia dracunculus

HEIGHT/WIDTH: $2' \times 1'–2'$ (60cm $\times$ 30–60cm)

FLOWERS/BLOOM TIME: tiny pale yellow panicles/
summer

ZONES: 4–9

RECOMMENDED USES: culinary

Tarragon

Beloved particularly by French chefs, this sharp, tangy herb is an essential ingredient in many recipes. It appears in the popular mixture known as *fines herbes*, along with parsley and chervil. Tarragon is also used in many delicious sauces, including béarnaise, hollandaise, and tartar, and is frequently added to mayonnaise, herb butter, and salad dressings. You'll want to try it in egg and vegetable dishes as well as with veal and poultry.

There are a few tricks to growing tarragon well. Begin with a seedling or cutting, as seeds are usually the similar-looking but coarser-flavored *A. dracunculus* var. *sativa* (Russian tarragon). Plant it in decent, well-drained soil, as it often struggles in damp sites and ground that is too acidic. If flowers appear, and they may not, clip them off to keep leaf production going. Tarragon has a tangled—to some eyes, "dragonlike" (hence the Latin name)—root system that requires division every couple of years to keep the plant vital. Mulch it to help it through cold winters.

The leaves are much tastier fresh than dried. Harvest them carefully so that you don't bruise them, and use them the same day if possible. You can also preserve them in white vinegar or freeze them. Dried sprigs lose their color and should be stored in an airtight jar to retain what flavor they do have.

Thyme

Thymus vulgaris

HEIGHT/WIDTH: 6″–12″ × 6″–12″ (15–30cm ×
15–30cm)

FLOWERS/BLOOM TIME: tiny, tubular, lavender to
pink/summer

ZONES: 5–9

RECOMMENDED USES: culinary

'Argenteus' thyme

Thyme is an absolutely charming plant, both for its history and for its beauty. It is also, of course, a great boon to cooks. There are many sorts of thyme, but the species remains the easiest to grow and the most popular. If you're curious, though, you might seek out lemon thyme (*T. × citri-odorus*), caraway thyme (*T. herba-barona*), or creeping thyme (*T. praecox* ssp. *arcticus*). Also check the tantalizing cultivars in the catalogs of herb specialists (see Sources).

Perhaps because its leaves and pretty, fragrant flowers are so tiny, thyme was once associated with fairies. In the Middle Ages, it was believed that if you ate certain dishes that featured thyme you would then be able to see the little folk. Gardeners also believed that fairies lived in thyme, and planted patches to provide shelter for them.

Modern-day gardeners may not reap these benefits but will nonetheless enjoy growing this useful herb. Its only requirement is well-drained soil, as the plant is vulnerable to root rot. However, thyme tends to become woody and raggedy-looking after a few seasons, and should be replaced with new plants. Provide winter protection, especially if your ground freezes.

Fresh or dried, thyme leaves are a wonderful asset to meats, poultry, game, shellfish, sausages, and vegetables, soups, and casseroles. The oil, once extracted, is called thymol and is found in cough medicines, mouthwashes, and other remedies, but can be dangerous in large quantities.

Turmeric

Curcuma domestica

HEIGHT/WIDTH: 12″–24″ × 6″–8″ (30–60cm ×
15–20cm)

FLOWERS/BLOOM TIME: pale yellow spikes/summer

ZONES: 9–10

RECOMMENDED USES: culinary, dye

Turmeric

A dramatic tropical plant best grown as a houseplant or in a greenhouse, turmeric is prized for its fleshy root, or rhizome. Until it is ready to harvest (at least several seasons), you will enjoy its beauty. Turmeric has large, lance-shaped leaves, up to 18 inches (45cm) long and 8 inches (20cm) wide. The flowers appear densely on spikes, and are a soft yellow with a tuft of white bracts at the tips.

To get this display, pot the plant in rich, moist soil and keep its atmosphere humid, either by raising it in a humid greenhouse or placing it on a tray of water and pebbles and misting it. Feed it occasionally during the growing season with a balanced houseplant fertilizer, and let it slow down in the winter months.

The root is yellow to deep orange and pleasantly fragrant. Dried and ground, it yields a bright powder that is used as a food coloring—most notably in common hot dog mustard and commercial curry powder. The root can also be soaked in water and the resulting liquid used to dye various fabrics yellow.

Valerian

Valeriana officinalis

HEIGHT/WIDTH: 2'–5' × 1'–2' (60–150cm × 30–60cm)

FLOWERS/BLOOM TIME: pale pink clusters/early
summer

ZONES: 4–8

RECOMMENDED USES: medicinal

Looks are deceiving with this pretty, clump-forming plant. The tall, graceful stems are lined with small, divided leaflets of toothed leaves, and are topped for weeks in the first part of the summer with dense little clusters of lovely white or lilac-pink blossoms that sway in the breeze. But be warned: its scent is, to some noses, unpleasant. The good news is that the strongest source is the root, so unless you dig up the plant, the scent may not trouble you. You should also know that while humans may not relish valerian's aroma, cats adore it, as do rats. In fact, legend has it that the Pied Piper of Hamelin lured the rats out of town by stuffing valerian in his pockets—the music was just for show.

The offending root, however, is also the plant's useful part. Valerian has a long history, and was used to treat everything from fevers to gastronomic distress. But its most famous uses are as a tranquilizer, depressant, and insomnia

Valerian

treatment for both humans and animals. These uses have been asserted as safe and effective by modern European researchers. You won't find it in medicines in the United States, however, because no drug company has yet put valerian through the paces that the FDA requires. Prolonged use or large doses have been reported to cause headaches, muscle spasms, and heart palpitations.

The plant will do well in full sun or partial shade, and prefers rich, moist, fertile soil. Harvest the roots in the autumn and use them in a cold or hot tea (one teaspoon to one pint [473ml] of water). Or dry the roots thoroughly and store in a moisture-free spot.

Wintergreen

Gaultheria procumbens

HEIGHT/WIDTH: *4"–6" × 4"–6"* (10–15cm × 10–15cm)

FLOWERS/BLOOM TIME: small white bells/summer

ZONES: 4–8

RECOMMENDED USES: medicinal, culinary

Wintergreen

Here's the source of that invigorating, penetrating scent we associate with cough and cold remedies, chewing gum, salves for sore muscles, and even real root beer. In recent times, true wintergreen has been replaced by synthetic imitations or the more easily extracted oil from black birch trees (*Betula lenta*). But for centuries, this little native North American plant was widely used.

Wintergreen is a hardy, creeping, groundcovering plant. The leaves are small, roundish, and glossy, and emit that wonderful menthol smell when broken or chewed. The equally fragrant roots may also be used and are best when freshly harvested. Extracting the oil from either is a long process that requires lots of plant parts, which is probably why it has been replaced by alternatives. For home use,

though, you can simply chop up some leaves as needed for a refreshing tea. In addition to relieving cold symptoms, the tea soothes an upset stomach and freshens your breath. A poultice makes a wonderful liniment or skin softener.

In nature, this plant thrives in moist soil on the forest floor under the dappled shade of high trees. So if you have an area in your yard with similar conditions, wintergreen will make a good groundcover. In addition to the glossy leaves, you can enjoy the appearance of small nodding white bell flowers that later yield round, bright red berries. Both the leaves and the berries remain over the winter months in many areas, and are a pretty and welcome sight.

Yarrow

Achillea millefolium

HEIGHT/WIDTH: 1½'–4' × 1'–2' (45–120cm × 30–60cm)

FLOWERS/BLOOM TIME: white, flat-topped/summer

ZONES: 3–10

RECOMMENDED USES: medicinal, craft, dye

Yarrow

Lacy-topped yarrow, with its thin, feathery, sage-green foliage, is an herb garden classic. Not only is it easy to grow—asking only full sun and fertile, well-drained soil—it is both pretty and useful. The species is white-flowered but is also available in pink, red, and violet, as well as mixes. Related species, such as *A. filipendulina* and *A. tomentosa*, extend the range into yellow, from pale pastel yellow to bold gold. All yarrows are long-blooming, so you can count on color from their corner of the garden all summer long. Plus, the flowers dry well, making them popular with flower arrangers and wreath makers. Harvest them at their peak and dry them upside down in a dark place. (Steeped in water, they'll yield a yellow dye.) The plants will often rebloom after an initial shearing.

As for medicinal uses, yarrow has been employed in a wide range of remedies. Perhaps its most enduring use has been as a poultice for wounds. (It allegedly gets its botanical name from the legend of the battle of Troy; apparently the hero Achilles used it to treat the injuries of his fallen comrades.) The modern-day discovery of various compounds in the plant that encourage blood clotting and act as anti-inflammatories validates this folk use. Other uses, such as treating fevers, acting as a diuretic, and easing indigestion, though not yet validated, continue to be practiced by some.

PLANT HARDINESS ZONES

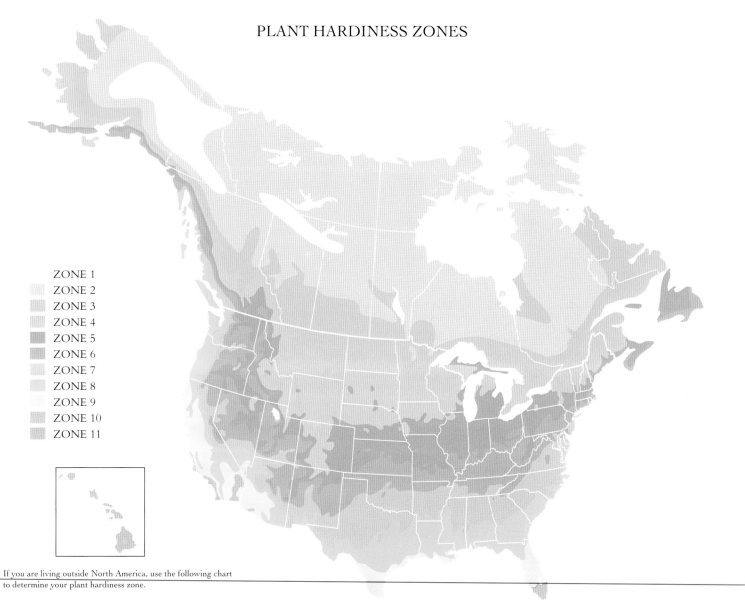

ZONE 1
ZONE 2
ZONE 3
ZONE 4
ZONE 5
ZONE 6
ZONE 7
ZONE 8
ZONE 9
ZONE 10
ZONE 11

If you are living outside North America, use the following chart
to determine your plant hardiness zone.

Range of Average Annual Minimum Temperatures for Each Zone

	Fahrenheit (°F)	Celsius (°C)
Zone 1	Below –50°	Below –45.6°
Zone 2	–50° to –40°	–45.6° to –40°
Zone 3	–40° to –30°	–40° to –34.4°
Zone 4	–30° to –20°	–34.4° to –28.9°
Zone 5	–20° to –10°	–28.9° to –23.3°
Zone 6	–10° to 0°	–23.3° to –17.8°
Zone 7	0° to 10°	–17.8° to –12.2°
Zone 8	10° to 20°	–12.2° to –6.7°
Zone 9	20° to 30°	–6.7° to –1.1°
Zone 10	30° to 40°	–1.1° to 4.4°
Zone 11	Above 40°	Above 4.4°

Sources

Here is a list of mail-order nurseries that specialize in herbs, or offer an especially broad selection. Note that many of these companies are small operations, and cannot afford to send out free catalogs, so please remember to include a check for the fee when requesting a copy.

Bluestone Perennials
7237 Middle Ridge Road
Madison, OH 44057
Free catalog

Companion Plants
7247 N. Coolville Ridge Rd.
Athens, OH 45701
Catalog $3

Filaree Garlic Farm
Rte. 2, Box 162
Okanogan, WA 98840-9774
Catalog $2

Goodwin Creek Gardens
P.O. Box 83
Williams, OR 97544
Catalog $1

Greenfield Herb Garden
P.O. Box 9
Shipshewana, IN 46565
Catalog $2

Herban Garden
5002 2nd St.
Rainbow, CA 92028
Catalog $1

Herbs-Licious
1702 S. Sixth St.
Marshaltown, IA 50158
Catalog $2

High Altitude Gardens
P.O. Box 1048
Hailey, ID 83333
Catalog $3

Le Jardin du Gourmet
Box 275
St. Johnsbury Center, VT 05863
Catalog $1

Logee's Greenhouses
141 North St.
Danielson, CT 06239
Catalog $3

Moonrise Herbs
826 G St.
Arcata, CA 95521
Catalog $1

Nichols Garden Nursery
1190 Old Salem Rd. NE
Albany, OR 97321
Free catalog

Plants of the Southwest
P.O. Box 11A
Santa Fe, NM 87501
Catalog $3.50

Rasland Farm
Rte. 1, Box 65C
Godwin, NC 28344-9712
Catalog $3

Richters Herbs
357 Hwy. 47
Goodwood, Ontario
L0C 1A0 Canada
Catalog $2

Sandy Mush Herb Nursery
Surrett Cove Rd.
Leicester, NC 28748-9602
Catalog $4

Tinmouth Channel Farm
Box 428B
Tinmouth, VT 05773
Catalog $2

Well-Sweep Herb Farm
205 Mt. Bethel Rd.
Port Murray, NJ 07865
Catalog $2

Westview Herb Farm
P.O. Box 3462
Poughkeepsie, NY 12603
Catalog $1

Wrenwood Nursery
Rte. 4, Box 361
Berkeley Springs, WV 25411
Catalog $2.50

Woodside Gardens
1191 Egg & I Rd.
Chimacum, WA 98325
Catalog $2

Here are some herb-related publications to subscribe to or seek out on the newsstand:

The Herb Companion
Interweave Press
201 E. 4th St.
Loveland, CO 80537-5655
bimonthly; $24/year ($31 Canada)

HerbalGram
P.O. Box 201660
Austin, TX 78720-1660
quarterly; $25/year ($30 Canada)

Herbs for Health
201 E. 4th St.
Loveland, CO 80537-9934
bimonthly; $24/year ($31 Canada)

Organizations to join:

Herb Society of America, Inc.
9019 Kirtland Chardon Rd.
Kirtland, OH 44094
Send a long SASE for information on dues and benefits

International Herb Association
P.O. Box 317
Mundelein, IL 60060-0317
Send a long SASE for information on dues and benefits

Canadian Sources:

Richters
Goodwood, Ontario/ L0C 1A0

Versey's Seeds Ltd.
York, Prince Edward Island C0A 1P0